BRIDGE BOOKS BY MARTY BERGEN

Better Bidding with Bergen, Volume One (1985)

Better Bidding with Bergen, Volume Two (1986)

POINTS SCHMOINTS! (1995)

More POINTS SCHMOINTS! (1999)

Negative Doubles (2000)

Introduction to Negative Doubles (2000)

MARTY SEZ (2001)

MARTY SEZ – VOLUME II (2002)

1NT Forcing (2002)

Evaluate Your Hand
Like an Expert (2002)

For information on ordering addition copies of this or other books, please refer to pages 207-210.

or call 1-800-386-7432

POINTS SCHMOINTS!

Bergen's Winning Bridge Secrets

By Marty Bergen

Edited by Patricia Magnus

Bergen Books
9 River Chase Terrace
Palm Beach Gardens, Florida 33418-6817

First Edition published 1995.
Printed in the United States of America.
10 9 8 7

First Printing: October, 1995
Second Printing: December, 1995
Third Printing: May, 1997
Fourth Printing: April, 1998
Fifth Printing: January, 1999
Sixth Printing: December, 2000
Seventh Printing: June, 2002

Library of Congress Control Number: 2002092454

ISBN 0-971663610

Dedication

To my wonderful parents, Florence and Jack:
I didn't always agree with you, but I never doubted
your love and support. Thanks for everything.

CONTENTS

ACKNOWLEDGMENTS

"Never has one author owed so much to so many."

Marty Bergen

Thanks To:

Kate Aker, Phillip Alder, Florence Bergen, Jack Bergen, Robert Bergen, Steve Bergen, Janet Bettman, Stacy Bettman, Bob Blanchard, Eileen Brenner, Laura Brill, Marvin Brown, Norman Buchnoff, Herb Cohen, Neil Cohen, Paul Cohen, Chris Cowles, Dennis Daley, Kirk Daley, Liz Davis, Susan Duval, Garland Ergruden, Shelley Fehrenbach, Cheryl Fischer, Rick Frishman, Stanley Goldberg, Charles and Mary Hill, Gert Hofheimer, Bob Howland, Zeke Jabbour, Terri and Walter Johnson, Peter Kalat, Larry King, Jonathan Kirsch, Naomi Klosner, Don Krauss, Sheryl Langer, Geraldine Lantz, Debra Larkin, Louis Lessinger, Janet Lippman, Scott London, Nancy Molesworth, Reed Morrill, Jim Munday, Richard Oshlag, Josh Parker, Dave Paull, Marvin Pulvers, John Rappaport, Diane Romm, George Rosenkranz, Susie Russenberger, Adrian Salee, Roberta Salob, Jane Salzberg, Lynne Schalman, Steve Schneer, Ginny Schuett, Sam Schwartz, David and Lisa Scroh, Doug Simson, Luella Slaner, Ken Smith, Mark Stafford, Jane Stern, David Straube, Frank Thomas, Jean René Vernes, Steve Weinstein, Roberta Whelan, Adam Wildavsky, Penny Zahn, Angelo Zuccaro, **and my students, who were happy to help me out**.

These Wonderful Books, and Their Talented Authors:

Have I Got a Story For You by Patty Eber and Mike Freeman

Classic Bridge Quotes by Jared Johnson

Harvey Penick's Little Red Book by Harvey Penick

5 Weeks to Winning Bridge by Alfred Sheinwold

The Official Encyclopedia of Bridge — Fifth Edition by Alan Truscott, Henry and Dorthy Francis

Bid Better, Play Better by Dorothy Hayden Truscott

My Very Special Thanks To:

Prolific Authors Dave Feldman, Eddie Kantar and Frank Stewart —

Your experience and expertise have proven invaluable.

Gracious Celebrities Omar Sharif and Zia Mahmood —

You helped make this special book even more special.

Computer Consultants Chyah and Kent Burghard —

You make hard drives seem easy.

Hard-Working Reviewers

Carole Bergen, Andy Bernstein, Susie Cohen, Lew Finkel, Barry Goldstein, Pat Harrington, Pat Hartman, Gregory LeMothe, Brent Manley, Chris Oakleaf, Al Romm, Nancy Sahlein and Bobbie Spellman —

You took my rough canvas and produced a work of art.

Marketing Advisors

Laurie Bergen, Joel Friedberg, Gladys Li, Donna Manley and Dick Mann —

Your guidance and wisdom helped me to forge ahead.

My A-Team

Cheryl Lantz Bergen, Larry Cohen
Jan Nathan, Steve Sahlein and Sue Smith —

Without you, my dream would still be on the shelf.
Simply the best!

My Ever-Present Editor

There is always one person without whom a book just could not go to press. A special thank you to my editor, Patty Magnus, for her help and industriousness – especially when we did not see eye to eye.

INTRODUCTION
In Pursuit of a Dream

DATELINE July 1962 — Solitary Confinement

At the tender age of 14, I was sentenced to a hospital for removal of a terrible set of tonsils. On her way to visit, my mother picked up a few books, to help the nurses and me survive each other. (For a healthy teenager, a three-day confinement in the hospital certainly qualifies as cruel and unusual punishment.) One book was a 50¢ paperback, *5 Weeks to Winning Bridge* by Alfred Sheinwold. I knew nothing about bridge, but had always enjoyed card games, starting with pinochle at my dad's knee as a precocious six-year old.

During my hospital stay, I devoured Sheinwold's book. Luckily for me, my non-bridge-playing mother had stumbled upon an absolute gem. I borrowed a deck of cards from the nurses, who were delighted with my new pacifier.

September 1965 — Classes No, Bridge Yes

Then came college, and what a revelation! Attendance in class was not mandatory. Bridge games were never-ending. Let me see, should I go to Accounting 101 or play some bridge? Not a tough decision.

My bridge game improved overnight. Unfortunately, my professors were unable to appreciate my skipping classes in pursuit of endplays and slams. When I went home for Christmas break, I was the not-so-proud possessor of a 1.0 GPA.

Meanwhile, I had been introduced to duplicate bridge. Winning masterpoints was much easier than passing exams. However, the following was now definitely in question: Would I graduate? If I did, which would come first, the required 120 credits or the 300 masterpoints needed to become a life master? Amazingly, the diploma preceded my gold card by almost six months.

June 1976 — Goodbye Nine-to-Five

My first published material, "That's No Bridge Player, That's My Wife," had previously appeared in *The Contract Bridge Bulletin*. In June 1976, I began writing monthly columns for that publication.

Ever since I decided to make bridge my life's work, I've had three goals. One was to win a national championship. On March 22, 1981, I finally broke through. The second was to win a world championship. Although I've been on the verge several times, that one still eludes me.

Goal number three was actually a dream. I've always wanted to write a practical, entertaining bridge book, the likes of which the world has never seen. What happened to my dream? I don't know; I always seemed to be busy with something else. However, I never forgot.

March 1994 — Helloooo Dream

The phone rings. It is my long-time friend and bridge partner, Larry Cohen. "Great news, Marty. Remember your idea for a classic bridge book? I just came across a book exactly like that."

"What's so great about that? I wanted to be the one to write that book. Nobody cares about who is second with a great idea!"

"No, Marty, you don't understand. It's a golf book. It represents the easy-to-read yet informative book that you've always talked about. Pick up a copy. It's called *Harvey Penick's Little Red Book*."

I viewed the wonderful Penick book as my sign from Above: "The time has come, Marty, to stop procrastinating." It had taken 18 years, but finally, I was on my way.

Fortunately, I didn't have to start from scratch. Like Penick, I have accumulated material from 20 years of teaching and playing. Many topics are a direct result of students' questions. Others are a product of their mistakes and confusion. I am very grateful; without them I could not possibly have written this book.

If you have only half as much fun reading this book as I've had writing it, my efforts will not have been in vain. Is there more to come? You better believe it. Am I interested in hearing your thoughts and questions? Absolutely!

Marty Bergen

CHAPTER 1
Opening Bids — Your Best First Move

"Points, Schmoints!" — Use the Rule of 20

"Players who count points and don't take note of distribution are a menace."

Terence Reese, legendary bridge player and writer

After teaching bridge for over 20 years, I thought I had seen it all. However, I had the following experience in the winter of 1994, and it made a lasting impression on me. My class consisted of 28 experienced players, and I will never forget that first hand. The dealer held:

♠ KQ54
♡ A873
♢ 6
♣ K1064

I was amazed as player after player passed this hand. Only one person opened 1♣. What was going on?

I immediately stopped their nonbidding and asked: "Do you open with 13 points?" Everyone answered yes. (Whew!) I now asked the $64,000 question. "How do you count your points when you pick up your cards?"

Seventeen students answered that they simply counted their high card points (HCP) and added points for distribution only *if* they found a fit!

Ten students answered that they added points for length to their HCP: one point for a five-card suit, two points for a six-card suit, etc. I am familiar with this technique, but I cannot agree with any method of evaluation that calls for passing hands like this one.

The one student who opened said that she was taught to add short-suit points to her HCP: one point for a doubleton, two for a singleton and three for a void. With 12 HCP plus two points for the singleton, she was happy to open. This was the technique I learned when I took up bridge.

How did I resolve the confusion? I taught them **The Rule of 20**.

In first and second seat, add the length of your two longest suits to your HCP. When the total is 20 or more, open the bidding. With less, do not open at the one level.

Here is how it works. It is a matter of simple addition:

HCP
+   # cards in longest suit
+   # cards in second longest suit

────────────────────────────────

Total

This is all you must know to determine whether you should open the bidding in first or second position (i.e., when partner has not had a chance to pass). If there is a tie for longest or second-longest, you can select either; I always use a major suit for my computation. Try some examples. The first is the hand that only one player opened in class.

1.   ♠ KQ54   12 HCP
     ♡ A873   4 spades
     ♢ 6   4 hearts
     ♣ K1064   ─────────────
                    20 — Open 1♣.

2. ♠ AQJ865   10 HCP
    ♡ —   6 spades
    ◇ 972   4 clubs
    ♣ K754   _____
                      20 — Open 1♠.

3. ♠ KJ5   12 HCP
    ♡ A875   4 hearts
    ◇ Q75   3 spades
    ♣ Q64   _____
                      19 — Pass.

4. ♠ 87   11 HCP
    ♡ Q54   7 diamonds
    ◇ AKQ9764   3 hearts
    ♣ 9   _____
                      21 — Open 1◇.

Counting points enables you to evaluate your trick-taking potential to bid to the correct contract. However, you cannot accurately assess your values if you count only HCP.

The reality of bridge life is that **hands with long suits and short suits have far more potential than their balanced counterparts**. Give The Rule of 20 a chance.

There is no question that The Rule of 20 will increase your chances of having an opening bid. Is this desirable? Here are my thoughts.

1. You bid more accurately after your side opens.

2. It is much easier to open than to overcall.

3. It must be right to get in the first punch. I hate to guess *after* my opponents have bid, particularly if they have preempted.

4. It is more fun to bid — absolutely, positively. If passing all afternoon is your idea of a good time, I suggest you check your pulse.

Not convinced? Try this problem:

	LHO	Partner	RHO	Dealer
♠ 63	—	—	—	P*
♡ AJ742	1♠	P	2♠	???
◇ 8				
♣ AJ943	* A point-counter. I hope you would know better.			

What now? To bid or not to bid, that is the question. If you decide to act, which suit do you bid? Wow, this is annoying.

What would I do? I would have opened 1♡ — based on The Rule of 20. Either you open at the one level or you guess later.

Perhaps the following will help. Distributional hands have stories that they would like to tell. For example:

♠ Q9842	11 HCP
♡ 7	5 spades
◇ AKQ8	4 diamonds
♣ 1094	
	20 — Open 1♠.

You	Partner
1♠ ("5 spades and enough to open")	2♣
2◇ ("4 diamonds")	2♡
3♣ ("3 clubs")	

Now partner knows it all. You are short in hearts. (5+4+3 leaves room for only one heart.) Well done! Don't you feel like taking a bow?

The Not-So-Short Club

"To me, the 'short club' is more of a bludgeon than a club, and one whose lethal effect is usually directed at one's self or one's partner."

Helen Sobel Smith, greatest woman bridge player of all time

Many players believe that an opening 1♣ bid is frequently based on a three-card suit. Others go even further and open 1♣ with only two cards in the suit when they have no attractive alternative. This is not my cup of tea. It is time to tell it like it is: **A player opening 1♣ usually holds four or more clubs**.

"An opening 1♣ bid is usually based on a three-card suit" is only one of many popular misconceptions. In addition, there are others that apply to rebids and responses after a 1♣ opening.

1. "Opener should rebid a five-card club suit to inform partner that he has a real suit." no, No, NO. If opener opens 1♣ and rebids 2♣ after partner's 1♡ response, he deserves to languish in his 5-1 *non-fit* when responder holds:

    ♠ A754   ♡ J8543   ◇ J65   ♣ 6

2. "You need five cards to raise opener's minor." Balderdash! Partner opens 1♣ and RHO overcalls 1♠. You are missing the boat if you would not raise to 2♣ with:

    ♠ 6   ♡ J74   ◇ Q8764   ♣ KQ106

3. "Respond up the line to a 1♣ opening." That is just fine when you have four hearts and four spades. I cannot see the slightest merit in responding 1◇ instead of showing your major with a hand like:

    ♠ 5   ♡ QJ76   ◇ QJ76   ♣ Q854

Bond Knows All the Tricks

All beginners learn to count their points, and they quickly become proficient at it. Unfortunately, you can become a slave to HCP. Good bidders know this secret:

> **Counting HCP alone is accurate only when bidding notrump with a balanced hand.**

The truth is that much more is involved in evaluating a hand than simply counting HCP.

Regrettably, old habits die hard. Many players are already deeply infected with "point countitis." The following entertaining hand cures some of them:

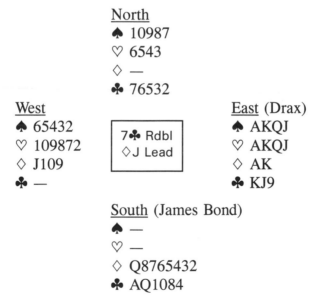

North
- ♠ 10987
- ♡ 6543
- ♢ —
- ♣ 76532

West
- ♠ 65432
- ♡ 109872
- ♢ J109
- ♣ —

7♣ Rdbl
♢J Lead

East (Drax)
- ♠ AKQJ
- ♡ AKQJ
- ♢ AK
- ♣ KJ9

South (James Bond)
- ♠ —
- ♡ —
- ♢ Q8765432
- ♣ AQ1084

Here is the incredible auction:

West	North	East	South
—	—	—	7♣!!
P	P	Dbl	Rdbl
All Pass			

I first encountered this remarkable hand as a teenager while reading Ian Fleming's *Moonraker*, a James Bond novel. Bond is hot on the trail of the evil Hugo Drax who, along with more serious vices, enjoys cheating at bridge. While the two are spending a lively evening at the bridge table, needling and jousting, Bond sets up this infamous hand. It is renowned in bridge lore as "The Duke of Cumberland hand."

Drax is given the imposing East cards, a point counter's dream come true. At this juncture in the evening, the betting between adversaries has become fierce, "one hundred fifty pounds a hundred, fifteen hundred pounds on the rubber, and a hundred pounds a trick on the side." Bond has pretended to be intoxicated in order to justify his 7♣ opening! Note: If West had guessed to take out the double, Bond might have become known as .007 — seven of either major is makable.

As you can see, dummy did not have much, but it was "exactly what the spy ordered." The ◊J lead was ruffed in dummy. However, no other lead would have affected the outcome. At trick two, Bond led a trump from dummy and covered East's nine with his ten. He ruffed another diamond, removing East's last honor. Another trump finesse followed, and all that remained was to pull East's trump king. Bond then led the ◊Q, capturing West's 10. All of Drax's honors were totally useless in the face of declarer's minor-suit winners!

The moral of the story is: **Point count is only one factor in hand evaluation**. Do not allow yourself to become dependent on it. No matter how many points you hold, high cards can always be neutralized by trumps and distribution. You can either accept this now, or you can join the "Draxes" of the world who learn the hard, expensive way.

Dear Marty: What Suit Should I Open?

Many players get confused when they are unable to open in a major. Which minor suit should they open? The stronger? The higher-ranking? The following guidelines answer these questions.

With **three cards in each minor** always open 1♣. Bidding a three-card suit is a lesser of evils. If you must, do so as cheaply as possible.

Deciding what to open with **four cards in each minor** is one of the most overrated of bridge players' concerns. With a balanced hand, open the stronger suit. If you have a singleton in one of the majors, open 1◇ unless your diamonds are very weak.

With **two five-card suits**, there is an important guideline: **Always open the higher ranking first**. However, even experts disagree about which suit to open with five spades and five clubs. The easy solution is to open 1♠, so that partner will immediately know that you have five cards in your major suit.

It is time to test yourself. Cover the answers on the right and decide what to open with each of the following:

1. ♠ AK5 ♡ Q864 ◇ A84 ♣ J32   1♣

2. ♠ AQ43 ♡ A54 ◇ KQ9 ♣ KJ3   1♣

3. ♠ K8 ♡ Q95 ◇ K743 ♣ AQ108   1♣

4. ♠ 7 ♡ 9743 ◇ KQ87 ♣ AK83   1◇

5. ♠ K ♡ A852 ◇ 8653 ♣ AQJ9   1♣

6. ♠ AJ765 ♡ 86 ◇ 5 ♣ AKJ54   1♠

7. ♠ 6 ♡ K4 ◇ A8652 ♣ KQJ97   1◇

Now you are ready for the next question. What do you open holding a balanced hand with 16–18 or 15–17 HCP and a five-card major?

Always Open 1NT — Even With a Five-Card Major

Whenever you have a balanced hand and the appropriate point count, open 1NT. **There are absolutely no exceptions. Do not be distracted by a five-card major.** Life will be much easier when you open 1NT with a five-card major and a balanced hand. You will not have a rebid problem, and your partner will immediately know about your strength and balanced distribution. If you open your five-card major, partner will not know about your strength now, and there will be no way to tell him later! Bridge can be a very unforgiving game: Either you open 1NT, or you forget about showing your 16–18 (or 15–17) HCP.

Although many regard the above as heresy, please read on. What would you open with this hand?

```
♠ 873
♡ KJ865
♢ AQ10
♣ AQ
```

If you open 1♡, your partner will often respond 1♠. The opponents are silent. It is time for your rebid; decide before continuing.

Let's round up the usual suspects, *oops*, I mean rebids:

1. Can you pass? Absolutely not! **Partner's 1♠ response did not deny a good hand.** It promised 6–16 points and was 100% forcing.

2. Can you rebid 1NT? No, this shows a balanced minimum; less than a 1NT opening. Obviously, a 1NT rebid misrepresents your strength.

3. Can you rebid 2♢? No. A 2♢ bid would promise a four-card suit. You are asking for trouble if you lie about your distribution.

4. Can you raise to 2♠? No. This shows a minimum hand with good spade support. Partner's response promises only a four-card suit.

5. Can you rebid 2NT? No. This shows more points than an opening 1NT bid. You would need about 19 points to make this bid.

Give up? You certainly do not need this aggravation — life is too short. Ignore your major and open 1NT.

♠ A10965
♡ KQ7
◇ Q7
♣ AJ4

It is true that partner will not know that you have a five-card major when you open 1NT with hands like these. That is not, however, the end of the world.[1]

It will be beneficial for you to declare a notrump contract. You would prefer to play last at trick one so that the lead does not come *through* your honors.

Here is a recap:

1. Should you still open 1NT if the major is strong? yes, Yes, YES.

2. Is this true regardless of which major is involved? yes, Yes, YES.

3. Should you open 1NT with *all* balanced hands that include a five-card major and have the appropriate strength? yes, Yes, YES.

Do I practice what I preach by always opening 1NT with five-card majors? Absolutely, positively, YES.

I'll conclude with two related examples.

What would you do as dealer with this hand?

♠ KJ765 ♡ AJ10 ◇ AQ ♣ KQJ   Open 2NT.

Your right-hand opponent (RHO) opens 1♠. What do you bid?

♠ KQ9 ♡ AJ765 ◇ AQ ♣ 875   Overcall 1NT.

Congratulations — you are on your way to becoming a practical, *nonstubborn* bridge player.

---

[1] A convention called Puppet Stayman allows responder to discover if opener holds a five-card major after opening 1NT.

The Spades Have It — The Rule of 15

After three passes, you are looking at a borderline hand. Should you open, or pass hoping that your next hand will be better?

The answer is to use The Rule of 15:

> **Fourth hand should open if your HCP plus number of spades totals 15 or more.**

Remember, this applies only to borderline hands; you know what to do with good ones.

Why are spades crucial here? You have limited strength and no one opened in front of you. You will therefore be waging a partscore battle in which you will want to outbid the opponents without getting too high. If you own spades, the opponents cannot buy the hand at the two-level.

Without spades, you might need to compete to the three level. The same is true for the opponents. If they want to compete over your 2♠ bid, their two passed hands do not rate to make a nine-trick contract. The more spades you have, the safer it is to open.

What suit should you choose for your opening bid? No problem! Open the bidding in the same suit you would have with a good hand.

Try the following examples to see how easy this is. Remember, add your HCP to the number of spades in your hand.

The auction has begun with three passes and you hold:

Open 1◇. 11 HCP + 4 spades = 15.

♠ AJ74
♡ K7
◇ K942
♣ 1063

♠ AQ965
♡ A87
◇ 52
♣ 943

Open 1♠. Use the Rule of 15. You have 10 HCP and five spades — a total of 15. You hope to make a low-level partscore.

♠ J2
♡ AQ965
◇ A87
♣ 943

Pass. With 11 HCP and two spades you should not open, even though this hand contains more HCP than the one above. You are concerned that the opponents hold spades, the dominant suit. Being able to make 2♡ is worthless if they can bid and make 2♠.

♠ Q
♡ KJ6
◇ A542
♣ Q8763

Pass. Your 12 HCP plus one spade total 13. Try your luck with some new cards.

♠ 73
♡ A873
◇ AKJ1064
♣ 2

Open 1◇. Only use The Rule of 15 when in doubt. With this lovely hand, you have no doubts.

Whether you are playing for masterpoints or the satisfaction of beating your friends, you prefer plus scores to minus scores. The Rule of 15 is a simple yet reliable tool to decide whether or not to open up what might prove to be a can of worms. You need not feel squeamish when armed with spades.

CHAPTER 2
Partner Opens 1NT — Now What?

Stayman Without Eight Points? Never Say Never

When partner opens 1NT and you are *short in clubs*, bid Stayman regardless of your point count — even with fewer than 8 HCP.

When players first learn Stayman, they are told, "At least eight points are needed to make the bid." Fine — when you are interested in game.

With this hand, it will be no fun watching partner suffer as he goes down in 1NT. Don't forget: The 1NT opener has limited options after Stayman. A 2♡ or 2♠ bid shows four hearts or four spades. A 2♢ bid denies a four-card major. Opener should never answer by bidding 2NT. Therefore, responder can bid Stayman without strength if he is prepared to pass opener's rebid. Respond 2♣ then pass at your next turn.

♠ 10875
♡ 9754
♢ 109832
♣ —

I am certainly not guaranteeing that you will take eight tricks with this garbage — that would be absurd. However, I will guarantee that you will take more tricks in a suit contract than you would in notrump.

Please keep in mind: **Stayman is an asking bid, not a telling bid.** The only time responder needs eight points is when he follows Stayman with a second bid.

When you bid Stayman with a weak hand that is short in clubs you are using *garbage (weak) Stayman*.

1. You respond 2♣;

2. Opener either bids his major or bids 2♢;

3. You pass, confident that you are in your best contract;

4. You relax as dummy and watch partner ruff his club losers.

Do you need precisely 4-4-5-0 shape to bid *garbage Stayman*? No, waiting for perfect hands is the sign of an impractical perfectionist. You should be delighted to *escape* from 1NT with each of these hands:

♠ Q108
♡ 9754
◇ J8632
♣ 7

Bid 2♣. At worst, you will play 2♠ with seven trumps and a singleton.

♠ 65432
♡ 9754
◇ A1097
♣ —

2♣ is correct. If partner bids 2♡, content yourself with a pass, but raise 2♠ to three — that extra trump is huge and worth a game invitation.

I have always had more fun bidding with weak hands than with strong ones. If partner opens 1NT and you are short in clubs, bidding Stayman — whatever your point count — is definitely a no-lose proposition.

"I Want to Bid Notrump" (Adapted from *Have I Got a Story for You*, by Patty Eber and Mike Freeman)

When I taught my wife Stayman, I explained that opener responds 2♡ or 2♠ with a four-card major. With no major, opener bids an economical 2◇. Those, I explained, were her only options. Unfortunately, my advice fell on deaf ears. The auction 1NT – 2♣ (me) – 2NT just kept happening!

I was friendly with a famous bridge teacher in our area, whom my wife greatly admired. As a last resort, I asked him to speak to her. He was sweet but direct. "Barbara, you may never again bid 2NT in response to Stayman. never, Never, NEVER."

The next time we played with friends, my beloved opened 1NT and I responded 2♣. She sat, and she shook and shivered and writhed, until finally a flash of inspiration lit up her face. Coyly she whispered, "3NT"!

Think Twice Before Revealing Your Secrets

Bid to exchange relevant information, never to advertise your assets.

♠ 74
♡ 53
♦ AKQJ104
♣ 974

Your partner opens 1NT. Whether this shows 16–18 or 15–17 HCP, you have enough for game, but not enough to consider slam. (We all know players who are always thinking about slam, but with this hand it would be quite a s-t-r-e-t-c-h.) What is your bid?

If you showed your diamonds, what were you hoping for? Let's play question-and-answer:

1. *Won't your diamonds sparkle in 3NT?*

   They sure will! You are providing six tricks.

2. *Will it be easier to take 11 tricks in diamonds than nine in notrump?*

   No, it will not. In 3NT, partner will only need to furnish three tricks, whereas in 5♦, he must provide five winners. When planning to bid game after partner's 1NT opening, avoid 5♣ or 5♦.

3. *Are you eager to become declarer?*

   No. Strive to conceal the stronger hand, allowing the 1NT opener to play last at trick one.

4. *What if opener lacks a stopper in one of your weak suits?*

   This is the biggest concern of many players. However...

   a) After partner opens 1NT with no diamond honors, he almost certainly has strength in each of the other three suits.
   b) Partner may make 3NT even without a stopper when neither opponent has five cards in your weak suit.
   c) The defenders are less likely to emerge with a killing lead after a non-revealing auction.

For those obsessed with showing off their 24-carat diamonds, here's a fanciful suggestion: Respond 3NT to make your partner (and me) happy. Before tabling your hand, stand up and announce, "I have gorgeous diamonds." That's one way to show your suit while bidding correctly.

However, be prepared to be shouted down. In most circles, the dummy is expected to produce 13 cards, not a speech.

If you are still tempted to tell all, take a look at the full deal:

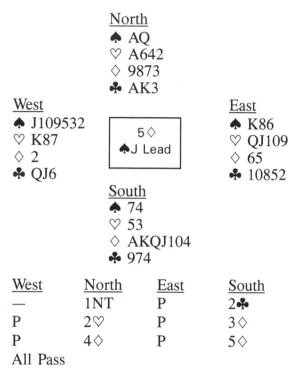

North
♠ AQ
♡ A642
◇ 9873
♣ AK3

West
♠ J109532
♡ K87
◇ 2
♣ QJ6

5◇
♠J Lead

East
♠ K86
♡ QJ109
◇ 65
♣ 10852

South
♠ 74
♡ 53
◇ AKQJ104
♣ 974

West	North	East	South
—	1NT	P	2♣
P	2♡	P	3◇
P	4◇	P	5◇
All Pass			

South's sequence of 2♣ (Stayman, at that point) followed by 3◇ is the method used by some players to show a very good hand with long diamonds. By showing his minor, responder is suggesting slam interest.

North was delighted to raise with four-card support and a maximum. He was less pleased when partner could not do anything interesting over 4◇. He was downright disappointed when the silly 5◇ contract failed.

The 11-trick game depended on the spade finesse, and after trick one, declarer was history. Meanwhile, 3NT would have afforded 10 of the easiest tricks ever seen. I hope that South will be more discrete next time, unless of course, I am his opponent.

CHAPTER 3
Not For Experts Only

21 Rules of Being a Good Partner

"I have always believed that your attitude toward your partner is as important as your technical skill at the game."

Rixi Markus, one of the all-time great players

Before you sit down to discuss what you are playing, you should start your partnership off on the right note. Half the battle of winning is being a good partner. Always observe the following:

1. Do not give lessons, unless you are being paid to do so. *"According to an evening paper, there are only five real authorities on bridge in this country. Odd how often one gets one of them as a partner."* Punch (British magazine).

2. Never say anything to your partner unless you would want him to say the same to you. If you are unsure whether your partner would want you to say something, don't.

3. Never "result" (criticize your partner for a normal action just because it did not work this time).

4. Unless your intent is to clear up a misunderstanding, avoid discussing the hand just played. If you cannot resist, be discreet.

5. Remember that you and your partner are on the same side.

6. Do not forget that your partner wants to win as much as you do.

7. If you feel the urge to be nasty, sarcastic, critical or loud — excuse yourself and take a walk.

8. When there is time between hands, do not discuss bridge.

9. When you want to consult another player about a disaster, ask about your hand, not your partner's.

10. Do not ever criticize or embarrass your partner in front of others.

11. Remember that bridge is only a card game.

12. Have a good time, and make sure that your partner does also. *"Bridge is for fun. You should play the game for no other reason. You should not play bridge to make money, to show how smart you are, or show how stupid your partner is... or to prove any of the several hundred other things bridge players are so often trying to prove."* Bridge legend Charles Goren.

13. Trust your partner; do not assume that he has made a mistake.

14. Although it may be unfashionable, it really is okay to be pleasant to a partner with whom you also happen to live.

15. Remember: *"The worst analysts and the biggest talkers are often one and the same."* Bridge columnist Frank Stewart. Think twice before verbally analyzing a hand. Do not embarrass yourself with a hasty, inaccurate comment.

16. When you voluntarily choose to play bridge with someone, it is not fair to get upset when partner does not play any better than usual.

17. Never side with an opponent against your partner. If you cannot support your partner, say nothing.

18. If you think you are too good for a partner, and do not enjoy playing bridge with him, do everyone a favor and play with someone else. That is clearly much better than being a martyr. However, be careful before burning bridges — another player's grass may not be greener.

19. Learn your partner's style, regardless of how you feel about it. Do not expect your partner to bid exactly as you would. When partner makes a bid, consider what he will have, not what you would.

20. Try to picture problems from partner's point of view. Seek the bid or play that will make his life easiest.

21. Sympathize with partner if he makes a mistake. Let your partner know that you like him, and always root for him 100%.

He Sure Talks a Good Game

"A man shouldn't oughtta open his mouth, unless he got a hand to back it up."

Cowboy on "Gunsmoke"

Everyone knows about major and minor suits. It is also clear what you are talking about if you refer to the black suits or the red suits. However, many players would be surprised if they overheard a player talking about his pointed suits!

Take a careful look at the shape of each of the four suit symbols. You will notice that the spades and diamonds have pointed peaks while the hearts and clubs are rounded. So much for that.

How about touching suits? Picture ♠ ♡ ◇ ♣. Touching refers to suits that are next to one another. ♠ and ♡ are touching, as are ♡ and ◇, and ◇ and ♣. The black suits, ♠ and ♣, are also considered touching.

What would you think if you overheard the following? "I held ace-queen fifth, king-jack fourth, stiff, three baby." Here are a few hints:

1. Describe hands in order of the suits, starting at the top: first spades, then hearts, then diamonds, then clubs. You don't need to identify the suits by name.

2. Small cards are not specified.

3. The number of cards in each suit is always stated.

4. "Stiff" is the accepted bridge slang for a singleton.

5. "Baby" represents small cards.

6. Strive for brevity. Therefore, the hand described is:

    ♠ AQxxx ♡ KJxx ◇ x ♣ xxx

"x" is the written designation for spot cards. If I were using a blackboard while teaching, I would write:

        AQxxx
        KJxx
        x
        xxx

The class would know that the suits were, in order going down the board: spades, then hearts, then diamonds, and finally clubs.

If you asked me what to bid with "Q975 of diamonds, the ace, king and three of clubs, the ace of spades, and my hearts were the king, jack, ten, eight and four," here's what would flash through my mind:

✓ I'm pleased you gave me your entire hand. A+. Very often, I am asked what to bid despite being told: "I had five diamonds including the ace and king and some nice spades."

✓ I'm also delighted that this hand contained 13 cards. If I had a quarter for every hand that I was given with an unusual number of cards, I would be a rich man. Another A+.

✓ You did a nice job identifying your high cards. I would have been happier if you had told me the number of cards in each suit. Also, you did not need to name your small cards. B+.

✗ I was not thrilled with the order in which I was given the suits. I had to make the effort to arrange the hand into spades, hearts, diamonds and clubs. D+ for this important category.

Overall, a very commendable B+. Got the idea? Try another hand.

"I opened 1NT with a 17-count. Three small, king-jack fourth, ace-king tight, ace-queen-ten fourth." Translation:

♠ xxx ♡ KJxx ◇ AK ♣ AQ10x

7. Number-count = HCP. For example: 16-count means 16 HCP.

8. "Tight" means only.

9. Middle cards (tens and nines) are named by the same players who have learned to appreciate them.

One more: "Ace doub, void, eight solid, three small."

♠ Ax ♡ — ◇ AKQJ10xxx ♣ xxx

10. "Doub" refers to a total of two cards, short for doubleton.

11. "Solid" indicates consecutive high honors beginning with the ace.

Impressing your peers may not be easy, but it is important. Not everyone can accomplish this with technique, but now that you can "talk the talk," you're on your way.

Thou Shalt Obey The Law of Total Tricks

How often have you been confronted with this classic situation? You are South and hear the following auction:

West	North	East	South
—	P	P	1♠
2♢	2♠	3♢	???

Some hands are easy; everyone should know to bid 4♠ here. This is *not* a 15-point hand.

However, suppose you held a more typical, nondescript opening bid such as one of these:

Your only decision is whether to compete to 3♠ or pass 3♢. What would an expert do?

The solution is so easy that anyone can learn to solve competitive problems effortlessly. It is based on the following: **When it comes to competitive bidding, trumps are everything.**

Simply count your trumps. Partner's raise to 2♠ promises three-card support. With the hand on the left you have five spades, so your side has a total of eight trumps.

Now ask yourself if your side's trumps are equal to the number of tricks needed to make your bid. If you bid 3♠, you would need to take nine tricks. You have only eight trumps, so you should pass.

With the hand on the right, you know your side has nine trumps. Therefore, it is correct for you to contract for nine tricks. Bid 3♠.

Do you know that you will take nine tricks with this hand? Of course not. You do not know whether partner has a minimum or a maximum.

However, it is clear that your sixth spade will only be an asset if spades are trump.

You may not realize this, but you already know something about the crucial concepts necessary to compete effectively. At some point in your bridge career, you were probably taught the following: It is correct to raise partner's 1♠ opening to 4♠ with a hand like this:

♠ K9865 ♡ 7 ◇ 96543 ♣ 84	*Points, schmoints!* This hand has great shape. Bid 4♠ — all day, every day! It was academic whether you could actually make 4♠. If you could not, the opponents were probably cold for 4♡. You took a sacrifice, consistent with *The Law of Total Tricks* ("The Law") which states:

> **You are safe in competing to the trick level equal to your partnership's number of trumps. Avoid bidding beyond that level in competitive auctions.**

Now use your knowledge of The Law to see how you would fare in these competitive bidding situations.

	LHO	Partner	RHO	You
♠ A8643 ♡ 4 ◇ 9654 ♣ 1087	1♣	1♠	2♡	???

Bid 4♠. Partner has at least five spades for his overall. 5+5=10. Bid to the 10-trick level.

	LHO	Partner	RHO	You
♠ Q863 ♡ A72 ◇ Q9 ♣ J642	— 3◇	1♡ P	2◇ P	2♡ ???

Pass. With only eight trumps, you are happy to let the opponents play at the three level. It will be easier to take five tricks on defense than nine on offense.

♠ A1054	LHO	Partner	RHO	You
♡ K865	—	1♡	2◊	2♡
◊ 73	3◊	P	P	???
♣ 632				

Bid 3♡ based on your extra trump. With a nine-card fit, you are justified in competing to the three level.

The Law is an essential ingredient for good bridge. It is easy to understand. Both you and partner know what to do based on your trumps. You will never again have to guess what to bid in competitive auctions such as these. Too bad all your bridge decisions will not be this easy!

After a frustrating afternoon of bad hand after bad hand, you pray that your luck has changed. However, when you pick up your cards, you are horrified — this hand is the worst of the lot. You are South and are looking at:

♠ 765432
♡ 2
◊ 5432
♣ 32

"Wow, no card above the seven! I have never seen a hand this bad. What did I do to deserve this? Watch your step, partner."

Your LHO deals and opens 1♡, which partner doubles. "What a pleasant development. Partner has a good hand with heart shortness. Things are looking up. I'm sure that we have a nice spade fit."

RHO raises to 4♡, which comes as no surprise. "Partner does not have hearts, and neither do I. That 4♡ bid takes me off the hook, I do not have to bid... But we do have a lot of spades." Here is a review:

West	North	East	South
1♡	Dbl	4♡	???

"I have six spades, and I expect partner to have four, a total of ten. The Law says that we are safe bidding to the four level with ten trumps." Either you believe or you don't. You bid 4♠ and are not surprised when West says, "Double."

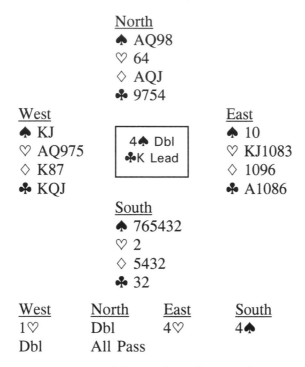

North
♠ AQ98
♡ 64
◇ AQJ
♣ 9754

West
♠ KJ
♡ AQ975
◇ K87
♣ KQJ

4♠ Dbl
♣K Lead

East
♠ 10
♡ KJ1083
◇ 1096
♣ A1086

South
♠ 765432
♡ 2
◇ 5432
♣ 32

West	North	East	South
1♡	Dbl	4♡	4♠
Dbl	All Pass		

East encourages a club continuation, and you ruff the third round. You finesse the ♠Q, and draw the remaining trump. You return to your hand by ruffing dummy's fourth club, and take the diamond finesse. Once you are back in your hand, you take a second diamond finesse. You score up your game, losing two clubs and one heart. Making 4♠ doubled!

Were you fortunate when both finesses won? Yes, although it was no surprise to find the two key kings in the opening bidder's hand. You certainly appreciated partner's ◇J.

You did not have to make your contract in order to justify the 4♠ bid. Going down one or two tricks would still net a profit compared to allowing the opponents to score up an easy game. Your 4♠ bid might even have pushed the opponents to the five level, which can't be bad.

You like points, I like trumps. *En garde!*

CHAPTER 4
Fits and Misfits

Sometimes the Fourth Suit is the Best Bid

```
♠ AJ5
♡ Q9754
◇ AK
♣ 832
```

You are pleased to pick up this nice hand and even happier when your partner opens 1◇. RHO passes and you respond 1♡. LHO also passes and partner rebids 1♠. Here is a review (with the opponents passing), allowing you to stall for time.

Partner	You
1◇	1♡
1♠	???

1. Should you bid 2NT? No. You would be promising at least one stopper in clubs. Why? When three suits have been bid, it is likely that the opponents will lead the unbid suit. **If the defenders have an indicated lead, declarer must be prepared for it**. It would be rash to jump in notrump without a club stopper.

2. Should you bid 3♡? This would be the choice of some players. Does it appeal to you? I hate it! A jump rebid in your own suit promises six of them. A suit like KQJ109 would be a reasonable exception, but Q9754, no way.

3. Should you bid 3♠? This bid has similar drawbacks; playing 4♠ with seven trumps will rarely be correct. Now what?

Note: Some experienced players would treat responder's second-round jump as invitational. Discuss this with your partner.

You are confident that you have enough strength to justify a game contract. However, at this point, it is impossible to know what that contract is. Let's look at some possible hands for partner, along with the appropriate final contracts:

(Hand repeated for convenience)

```
♠ AJ5
♡ Q9754
◇ AK
♣ 832
```

1.   ♠ K864 ♡ A ◇ QJ974 ♣ A109   3NT looks fine.

2.   ♠ Q872 ♡ AJ3 ◇ J972 ♣ AJ   4♡, obviously.

3.   ♠ Q863 ♡ K2 ◇ QJ8743 ♣ A   5◇.

4.   ♠ KQ73 ♡ AK ◇ QJ9762 ♣ 4   6◇ is cold.

As you see, there are many possible contracts. You need to choose the bid that is most flexible, allowing partner to describe his hand.

Good news — not only is this not a nightmare, it is not even a problem. The solution for responder with good, flexible hands is to bid *fourth-suit game forcing*. By the way, for those who play duplicate, the bid requires an alert.

Suppose partner has hand number two above.

Partner	You
♠ Q872	♠ AJ5
♡ AJ3	♡ Q9754
◇ J972	◇ AK
♣ AJ	♣ 832

Your auction will be:

Partner	You
1◇	1♡
1♠	2♣*
2♡	3♡
4♡	Pass

* Game-forcing, says nothing about clubs

Responder's bid in the fourth suit announces:

1.   "I also have a good hand, with an opening bid of my own."

2.   "We must bid to game (or slam)."

3.   "My bid says nothing at all about the suit named. It is an artificial bid, just like Stayman."

Therefore:

4.   Opener should continue to describe his hand.

5.   If opener bids notrump, he must have a stopper in the fourth suit.

Quite a mouthful! *Fourth-suit game forcing* tells partner about your good hand, while preserving all options.

Here is one more for the road.

♠ A54
♡ 963
♢ AJ753
♣ A2

The auction has proceeded (opponents silent):

Partner	You
1♣	1♢
1♠	???

Déjà vu. Bid the fourth suit — 2♡. You have no plausible alternative, which is why this convention is a vital element in your bidding arsenal.

It is difficult to reach the best contract when auctions begin with bids in three different suits. *Fourth-suit game forcing* will help solve your second-round bidding guesses and enable you to bid accurately. If anyone makes you a better offer than that, grab it, but please make sure to read the fine print very carefully.

Beware the Misfit

> *"Sometimes the bulls win. Sometimes the bears win. But the hogs* ***never*** *win."*
>
> *Wall Street Adage*

It would be nice if your side had a good fit on every hand, but life is not like that. Here is a remedy:

When you sense a misfit, stop bidding ASAP.

Do not fight with your partner. Stubbornness can cost you points — lots of points. Does this scenario look familiar?

West	East
♠ Q752	♠ K4
♡ 7	♡ KJ9854
◇ AK1032	◇ 84
♣ AJ7	♣ Q62

West	North	East	South
1◇	P	1♡	P
1♠	P	2♡	P
2NT	P	3NT	Dbl
All Pass			

What went wrong? 3NT doubled was carnage — down four! East's 2♡ bid was correct; it showed a six-card heart suit and a weak hand. If East had held only five hearts, he would have passed 1♠, bid 1NT, or taken a preference to diamonds. East thought that 2NT invited 3NT, and was delighted to accept the invitation with his 9 HCP.

The culprit was West. He had a nice hand; however, he should have been turned off when partner showed a weak hand with hearts. Bidding 2NT was 100% wrong. Although many players fall into this trap, **2NT is never a rescue bid**.

The following guidelines should have helped West pass 2♡.

1. Unless the hands have great combined strength, the worst place to play a misfit is in notrump.

2. Try to avoid notrump contracts when you have a singleton or void.

3. Good notrump contracts require more than stoppers. They must also contain a source of tricks. (Stoppers may prevent sudden death, but they will not ensure long life.)

Discipline yourself to *pass*, even when you are uneasy about your fit. In fact, **you should go out of your way to pass without a fit.** You may be reluctant to declare with seven trumps, but keep the following in mind:

a) A 2♡ contract requires only eight tricks.
b) If 2♡ does go down, *no double no trouble.*
c) The 2♡ contract is as good as any and is likely to make. At worst, East will lose the ♠A, one club and three trump tricks.

Here is another example.

♠ AQ653
♡ 8
♦ A865
♣ A96

You open 1♠ and your partner responds 1NT. You don't care for notrump so you rebid 2♦. Partner counters with 2♡. Now what?

1. Should you rebid 2♠? No, you have already said that your hand contains five spades.

2. Should you rescue with 2NT? No, 2NT is never a rescue bid.

3. Should you pass? Yes, you must. You have already described an opening bid with spades and diamonds. After partner rejects your suits and proposes his own candidate, you should throw in the towel. Partner's 1NT response to 1♠ did not *deny* a long suit. What else could he do without the 10 points needed to respond 2♡ over 1♠?

Partner	You
♠ 2	♠ AQ653
♡ J109632	♡ 8
◇ K43	◇ A865
♣ K53	♣ A96

The correct auction:

Partner	You
—	1♠
1NT	2◇
2♡	Pass

In 2♡, partner is able to succeed without a struggle, losing one club, one diamond, and three trump tricks.

There are times when your side is unable to agree on a suit. As soon as this happens, stop bidding. It is better to play a misfit at a low level than bid on and arrive at a ridiculous game contract. Sensible souls will keep in mind: "When the hands don't fit, it's time to quit."

Don't Be Shy, Tell Me What You Prefer

Sitting South, you are dealt the following mediocre hand:

	West	North	East	South
♠ KQ643	—	1♡	P	1♠
♡ 103	P	2♣	P	???
◇ J1093				
♣ J5				

What is your call?

1. Should you pass? Do not panic, passing 2♣ is not the answer. Four-two fits are not the solution, even when you are stuck.

2. Should you bid 2◇? No, a new suit by an unpassed responder is forcing. The last thing you want with this weak, misfitting hand is to *force* partner to do more bidding.

3. Should you bid 2♠? No way. You should not rebid an unsupported five-card suit. Once partner bids hearts and clubs, he is likely to hold a singleton spade. 2♠ takes you from the frying pan into the fire.

4. Should you bid 2NT? No, **2NT invites partner to bid 3NT if he has more than a minimum opening bid**. You would need about 11 HCP for an invitational 2NT bid.

There is an answer to this dilemma. The absolutely correct action for responder (drumroll please) is a *preference bid* of 2♡. This bid does not promise any strength — it is neither a new suit nor a jump. You are sure that your side has more hearts than the opponents, which may not be the case if you were to play in clubs or spades.

Will partner think you have three hearts and bid on? He should not. If you really *liked* hearts, you would have supported them immediately.

A preference shows no more strength than a pass, and is very often the key to avoiding trouble.

A Unique, Crucial Exception

"It is a miracle to me that, in all the literature of bridge, there is not a single chapter on 'how to pass.'"

Ely Culbertson, outstanding pre-Goren bridge personality

A new suit by responder is 100% forcing as long as he is an unpassed hand and the auction is not competitive. Understanding this is crucial to harmonious partnership bidding. The only exception occurs after opener rebids 1NT.

♠ J9754	Opener	Responder
♡ KJ864	1◇	1♠
◇ J6	1NT	???
♣ 5		

Responder must be allowed to escape from notrump with this hand. Therefore, **after opener rebids 1NT, a new suit by responder (in a lower ranking suit than responder's first bid) is nonforcing and shows a weak, distributional hand.** A 2♡ rebid by responder on this auction shows five spades and four or five hearts. It asks opener to express a preference between spades and hearts at the two level.

1. With four hearts, opener will usually be content to pass. With a maximum, he can raise to 3♡.

2. If opener does not have four hearts, but does have three spades, he will bid 2♠, taking a preference to the 5-3 spade fit.

3. With two spades and three hearts, opener has a choice. He will pass 2♡ with heart strength; otherwise he will bid 2♠.

With a better hand, responder would make a forcing bid. Discuss what bids *would* be forcing on this auction with your partner.[1]

---

[1] Many experienced players use an artificial bid similar to Stayman to ask opener about major suits in this sequence. Two of the more popular conventions are *new minor forcing* and *checkback Stayman*.

CHAPTER 5
The Battle of the Sexes

Unleashing Hostility
"We believe that the bridge table is used as a socially acceptable place to get rid of frustrations in a marriage."

Jim and Lois Scott, West Coast bridge couple

Not Just Anatomically Different
"A woman's inner sense of value tells her that bridge is not really a matter of life and death, but a man, whose ego is at stake, is a much harder fighter and treats bridge as a challenge to his mentality."

Anonymous

Woman Bridge Pro
A female bridge professional graciously agreed to donate her services for a charity event. Her partner was nice enough, but it would be fair to say that bridge was not his game. Late in the evening, he excused himself and headed for the men's room. The hostess asked the pro how they were doing. "My partner is a charming gentleman, but to be perfectly honest, this is the first time all night I know what he has in his hand!"

Husbands and Wives
In an elevator at a tournament, a man and a woman were arguing about the play of a bridge hand. Someone asked them if they were married. "Of course," the woman answered, "do you think I would live in sin with an idiot like that?"

Teaching Your Spouse
"A husband should never try to teach his wife to play golf or drive a car. A wife should never try to teach her husband to play bridge."

Harvey Penick's Little Red Book

Chivalry is Not Dead

*"Bridge is essentially a social game, but unfortunately it attracts
a substantial number of antisocial people."*

Alan Truscott, bridge editor of The New York Times

Picture the following: I was playing duplicate bridge against a couple who ended up in a ridiculous contract, doubled and vulnerable to boot. Mr. Smith did not look pleased during the auction, but completely lost it when his hapless wife tabled her dummy. Mr. Smith then proceeded to vent his spleen at his better half. Although no one would have criticized her for retaliating, she burst into tears and ran off.

Boorish behavior is never justified, but it was especially ironic in this case. Mrs. Smith's bidding had been totally reasonable. In fact, if I were serving as judge and jury, my only criticism would have concerned her choice of partner/spouse.

My partner and I were able to quiet things down a little, although the whole room continued to stare at the table where there were now only three players. We managed to finish the hand, and went plus 800.

I would like to have said something to defend the innocent victim. Unfortunately, Mr. Smith was the size of a mobile home. There had to be some clever tactic. What would Confucius say?

And then it came to me. "Angry man fight, smart man write." I ripped off a corner of my convention card and scribbled the following: "Your bidding was 100% correct."

When Mrs. Smith returned, I waited until Moose was studying his cards, and discreetly slipped my message under her convention card. She said nothing, but her smile was worth a thousand words.

Mixed Pairs — Everyone's Favorite Event

"If you feel that you absolutely must play bridge with your husband or wife, I propose this rule. Each time you pick up a hand, slowly and fervently intone to yourself: No matter what happens on this deal, I won't get angry. And stick to it. Who knows, you might both get home that night in a pleasant frame of mind."

Helen Sobel Smith

And now for the *pièce de résistance.*

A Deadly Game of Bridge

> *"Husbands and wives make poor partners — unless they happen to be someone else's husband or wife."*
>
> *Milton Ozaki, bridge writer*

In many respects, the most disastrous bridge hand ever played took place in Kansas City, Missouri on September 29, 1929. The ill-fated victim was 36-year-old John G. Bennett, a prosperous perfume salesman. According to the police report, he met his demise because he failed to make a bridge hand.

John and his wife Myrtle were playing bridge against another married couple, Charles and Mayme Hoffman. The Bennetts had been arguing all evening, but the situation came to a head when Mr. Bennett failed to make a 4♠ contract. Mrs. Bennett violently castigated her husband, which provoked him into announcing that he would spend the night in a hotel, and then leave town. As the Hoffmans started to leave, Mrs. Bennett took the family pistol from her mother's room and shot her husband. He staggered to a chair uttering the words "She got me." On arrival, the police found Mrs. Bennett weeping over the body.

Mrs. Bennett was tried for murder in March 1931 and acquitted! How was that possible?

Legend has it that:

1. Mrs. Bennett had an excellent attorney.

2. Mrs. Bennett was extremely attractive and the jury was male.

Got the picture?

Here is the allegedly fatal hand:

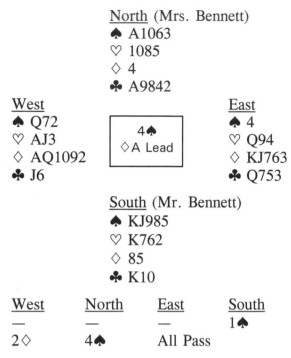

North (Mrs. Bennett)
♠ A1063
♡ 1085
◇ 4
♣ A9842

West
♠ Q72
♡ AJ3
◇ AQ1092
♣ J6

4♠
◇A Lead

East
♠ 4
♡ Q94
◇ KJ763
♣ Q753

South (Mr. Bennett)
♠ KJ985
♡ K762
◇ 85
♣ K10

West	North	East	South
—	—	—	1♠
2◇	4♠	All Pass	

Mr. Bennett opened the bidding with less than traditional values, and his wife took a shot (sorry about that) at game with a jump to 4♠.

Mr. Bennett actually took a reasonable line of play. West led the ◇A and shifted to the ♣J. South won the ♣K and cashed the ace and king of trumps. With the actual distribution, he was unable to make the hand.

Mr. Bennett could have succeeded if he had known that West had the ♠Q by finessing and drawing trumps. He would then have cashed the ♣A, and taken a ruffing finesse by leading the ♣9, then the ♣8, through East's queen. The ensuing two club winners would allow declarer to dispose of two hearts. He would lose only two heart tricks, along with the initial diamond. Sometimes, a finesse can be a life-saver!

"A not-surprising aftermath of the Bennett case was that Mrs. Bennett found it exceedingly difficult to find bridge partners."

Ron Klinger, prolific Australian bridge writer

CHAPTER 6
Cuebids: "Michaels Row Your Boat Ashore"

Seven Bills; I Mean B-I-G Bills

> *"The difference between genius and stupidity is that genius has its limits."*
>
> *Anonymous*

I called up my longtime friend and bridge partner, Larry Cohen. "L.C., I've got a story even you won't believe."

"Marty, I'd believe any story about you at the bridge table!"

"I went for seven *bills*." [Editor's note: Usually a $100 bill.]

Larry knows that I'm a very aggressive bidder, and sometimes this approach does not work. Our conversation took place in the early 1980s before the scoring chart was changed. In those days, down four doubled, not vulnerable, was a penalty of 700 points. An article in *The Bridge World* even suggested that one reason for the change in scoring was to penalize my outrageous preempts at favorable vulnerability!

"Seven bills," said Larry, "that's no big deal — unfortunately, I've seen you go for more than that."

"No, Larry, they were *very big* bills."

I was playing in a tournament with a student and picked up my kind of hand: not many high cards, but a lot of shape.

Both sides were vulnerable. I was South and my exact hand was:

	West	North	East	South
♠ J	2♣	P	2♠	???
♡ Q108743				
◇ —				
♣ 976542				

The 2♣ bid promised a very big hand, and was artificial, unrelated to clubs. The 2♠ bid was a positive response, promising a good five-card spade suit with at least 8 HCP. It sounded as if the opponents were on their way to slam, and two thoughts came to mind:

1. The opponents' auction was open to preemption. The 2♣ bidder had not yet said anything about his distribution, and I wanted to make it as difficult as possible for him to do so.

2. I wanted to suggest a sacrifice to partner. If the opponents could make a grand slam, I had a lot of latitude.

Of course, it would be crucial for our side to play in our best suit. How could I preempt while telling partner about my two suits? Aha, good old Michaels...

The most popular convention for two-suited hands is the *Michaels cuebid*. If your RHO opens 1♣ or 1◇, a cuebid of two of his minor promises at least five cards in each major. If your opponent opens in a major, a cuebid promises the unbid major plus one minor. *Voilà!*

I cuebid responder's spades, expecting partner to realize that I held a two-suited hand with hearts and a minor. If partner needed to discover my minor, a bid in notrump would force me to reveal it.

However, I was not content with a simple 3♠ cuebid. No one enjoys preempting more than I do, so I jumped to 4♠! I could not possibly be showing spades; after all, my RHO had already announced length and strength in that suit.

My partner was an experienced player, and I expected him to get the message. There was not any risk (famous last words). Even if partner left me in spades, I could always run after the opponents doubled. They would have to double; defeating the undoubled contract would not compensate them for their slam even if they took all 13 tricks!

My LHO gave me a "we-don't-bid-that-way" look, and bid 4NT. When his partner responded 5♢, he continued with 6♢, showing his suit. He could have rebid 5NT, which would have:

1. Confirmed all the aces;

2. Asked partner for his number of kings;

3. Invited partner to bid seven with extra winners. (Many players are unaware of this.)

"Let me see, what should I lead?" Wait, the auction was not over. To my complete shock, partner now emerged with a 6♠ bid. I cannot imagine how many spades he thought I had when he held five of them and his LHO had shown at least five.

East (RHO) doubled, and it was now time to retreat. Redoubling for rescue (*SOS*) may have occurred to some; how could I want to play in 6♠ redoubled after West opened 2♣ and East showed spades? However, I was unwilling to risk playing there; after all, if partner thought I had spades (and it appeared that he did), he might pass!

Not wanting to emphasize clubs, I ran to 6NT; partner must know that I did not want to play there! "M-a-r-t-y, you're f-o-r-g-e-t-t-i-n-g, never make a $1 bid with a 50¢ partner." Of course, my 6NT bid was also doubled. Now I should clearly have bid 7♣ (only down four).

Unfortunately, I wanted to be flexible, and took one of the most impractical, naive and costly (some would add idiotic and moronic) actions in the annals of bridge. I redoubled for rescue!

When everyone passed, I had gotten what I deserved. How about applying the KISS system, Marty? Keep It Simple, Stupid! Here is that memorable auction.

West	North	East	South (Marty)
2♣	P	2♠	4♠
4NT	P	5♢	P
6♢	6♠	Dbl	6NT
Dbl	P	P	Rdbl
P	P!	P	

And now for the result that will never be duplicated:

North
♠ 97542
♡ K5
◇ 932
♣ Q108

West
♠ A3
♡ A6
◇ AKQJ854
♣ KJ

| 6NT Rdbl |
| ◇A Lead |

East
♠ KQ1086
♡ J92
◇ 1076
♣ A3

South (Marty)
♠ J
♡ Q108743
◇ —
♣ 976542

West	North	East	South
2♣	P	2♠	4♠
4NT	P	5◇	P
6◇	6♠	Dbl	6NT
Dbl	P	P	Rdbl
P	P!	P	

Observe the lead of the ace from AK. This is a popular modern convention which I recommend.

There was not much to the play; after all, the opponents were entitled to 15 tricks. I conceded immediately, down 12! Although there was uncertainty in calculating the score, we eventually concluded that the number was a nice, round 7000.

Bridge hands come and go. Certainly no one can win them all. However, the deal on which I lost more points than the number of dollars I spent straightening both my kids' teeth is one I shall never forget.

Cuebids, No More Dangerous Than Dynamite

"The road to hell is paved with good conventions."

Anonymous

One of the most intriguing learning opportunities for an aspiring bridge player is the playing lesson. The many benefits of sitting across the table from an expert include:

1. The enjoyable experience itself. Don't you prefer partners who play better than you do?

2. The opportunity to receive prompt, accurate answers to all of your bridge questions.

3. An objective evaluation of your bridge game.

Unfortunately, some players assume that being partnered by an expert guarantees success. Not so. *A chain is only as strong as its weakest link* comes to mind here. Too often, the professional can only sit and watch as the student learns some valuable lessons the hard way

One concept that is difficult for players to unravel is the cuebid. Recently I was involved in another potential cuebid disaster. (Could it be me?) However, on this occasion, fate chose to smile on us — with a little help from an opponent.

Let me present this hand from partner's point of view. We were vulnerable, and she held...

```
♠ K10876
♡ A9743
♦ —
♣ 854
```

... and heard the auction proceed 1NT – P – 2◊* (alert). Christine (not her real name) did not care about the alert. All she knew was that she held both major suits and the opponents had bid. She was bursting to show her teacher how well she had learned her lessons regarding the *Michaels cuebid*.

To review, the *Michaels cuebid* is an important modern convention. When RHO opens the bidding, a cuebid promises a two-suited hand with at least five cards in each suit. Point count is secondary, as it should be. The suits should be strong enough to withstand disaster if partner does not have a fit with either of them.

Christine was much too excited to concern herself with details. She knew that it was correct to cuebid 2♢ with the majors if her RHO opened 1♢; so, how could it be wrong to cuebid 3♢ over 2♢? However, in this auction, the 2♢ bid did not show diamonds. Instead, it promised hearts. This was a *Jacoby transfer*, another popular modern convention. Although she did not realize it, Christine's 3♢ bid was *not* a cuebid. Cuebids are made only in suits in which the opponents have promised length. She was making a natural overcall in diamonds.

I should take a moment to point out that there was an opportunity for a *Michaels cuebid* in this auction. If Christine had held spades and a minor, she could have cuebid 2♡, the suit promised by responder.

3♢ was doubled by the notrump bidder, and two passes followed. Here is a review of the bidding:

Opener	Marty	Responder	Christine
1NT	P	2♢*	3♢
Dbl	P	P	???

* *Jacoby transfer* showing at least five hearts.

Christine was surprised when I did not select a major after her *cuebid*, but fortunately, she did realize that the bidding wasn't over. She certainly did not want to play in her void, so she bid 3♡.

What happened next? Take a look:

North (Christine)
♠ K1087
♡ A9743
◇ —
♣ 8654

West
♠ 96
♡ QJ852
◇ KQJ
♣ Q109

| 3♠ Dbl |
| ◇K Lead |

East
♠ AQ4
♡ K106
◇ A9842
♣ K3

South (Marty)
♠ J532
♡ —
◇ 107653
♣ AJ72

West	North	East	South
—	—	1NT	P
2◇*	3◇!	Dbl**	P
P	3♡	Dbl***	3♠
P	P	Dbl****	All Pass

*   2◇ was alerted, but Christine didn't ask.
**   You could hear this double in the next room.
***   You could hear this double in the next state.
**** You could barely hear this double at the table.

I was surprised when East doubled Christine's 3◇ overcall. However, I was not shocked, because these eyes have seen, and ears have heard — everything. After Christine's 3♡ bid, it became clear that she had been attempting to show the majors, so I retreated to spades. I was hopeful; four trumps, an ace and a void felt good opposite a hand that was worth a vulnerable cuebid at the three level. East's double of 3♠ was far from exuberant, but West ethically passed.

Did you notice that the North hand changed from the one that I described earlier? That was not a typo. Christine had proudly tabled 5-5 in the majors; unfortunately the ♠6 was actually the ♣6.

"Oh no," she giggled as I suggested that she move her small spade in with her clubs. "At least, it wasn't the king."

"Thank you, partner, you do have an interesting hand."

(Deal repeated for convenience)

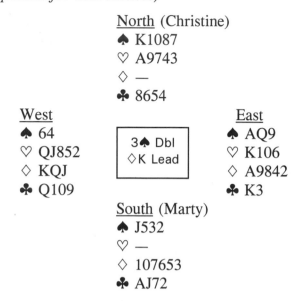

North (Christine)
♠ K1087
♡ A9743
◇ —
♣ 8654

West
♠ 64
♡ QJ852
◇ KQJ
♣ Q109

3♠ Dbl
◇K Lead

East
♠ AQ9
♡ K106
◇ A9842
♣ K3

South (Marty)
♠ J532
♡ —
◇ 107653
♣ AJ72

Here's the play in 3♠ doubled:

Trick 1:   Ruff the ◇K opening lead in dummy with the ♠7.
Trick 2:   Lead the ♣4 to the ace.
Trick 3:   Trump the ◇5 with dummy's ♠8.
Trick 4:   Cash the ♡A, discarding the ♣2.
Trick 5:   Ruff the ♡3 in your hand with the ♠2.
Trick 6:   Ruff the ◇6 in dummy with the ♠10.
Trick 7:   Ruff the ♡4 with the ♠3.
Trick 8:   Lead the ◇7, trumping with dummy's ♠K.
Trick 9:   Play the ♡7 from dummy. East finally interrupts the crossruff
           by trumping in with the ♠A. The ♠J5 guarantees a ninth trick.

Plus 730 (duplicate scoring) certainly was a great result for us. East berated West for not finding a trump lead, which would have been correct (the analysis, not the behavior).

Not surprisingly, the last word belonged to Christine. "You were right, Marty, Michaels is a wonderful convention!"

CHAPTER 7
Doubles Anyone?

Saved by Marty (A Story by Larry Cohen)

"The real test of a bridge player isn't in keeping out of trouble, but in escaping once he's in."

Alfred Sheinwold, well-known syndicated bridge columnist

Sitting across the bridge table from Marty Bergen for more than a decade has provided many memorable moments. We have had our ups (seven national championships), and our downs (two heart-breaking losses in playoffs to qualify for the world championships). We have had controversy (some historic committee rulings), and scares (the kidnapping of our teammate's wife while we were playing).

Marty's aggressive bidding style was usually successful, but every now and then I'd have to enter minus 1100 on our scorecard. Marty always loved to jump when our side found a trump fit. On a deal from the 1986 national championships in Atlanta, Marty jumped, and I was ready to write in a huge minus score. Here's my tale of an unforgettable deal.

Playing in the finals of the prestigious Blue Ribbon Pairs, with both sides vulnerable, I held:

```
♠ J973
♡ Q82
♢ —
♣ KQ9873
```

Our table was packed with kibitzers, as we were among the leaders in the event. Marty dealt and opened 1♢, which was followed by a takeout double.

Without the double, I would have responded 1♠; I did not have enough points to show my clubs at the two level. However, after a double, 10 points are no longer required for a two-over-one response. In fact, most players treat this response as nonforcing.

Rather than bid my meager spades, I decided to show my longest suit, so I responded 2♣. Marty alerted. (In duplicate bridge, partner "alerts" an artificial call to let the opponents know the bid is not natural and to allow them to ask about the meaning.)

Oh-oh. What is this alert? Immediately a feeling of horror spread from my head to my stomach. This was a new convention (yet another Bergen brainchild) in which 2♣ did *not* show clubs. The opponents asked Marty what my bid meant.

I now woke up and remembered our agreement. After our opening 1◇, 1♡ or 1♠ is doubled, responder's 2♣ bid is artificial. The bid says nothing about clubs, but promises a decent raise to two of opener's suit. An immediate raise to 2◇ after the double would have shown a very weak hand, roughly 6–7 points. My actual 2♣ bid was supposed to have shown support with 8–10 points.

Well, I had the eight points, but one might take issue with my "support." Marty explained my bid to the opponents, and all I could do was listen. Nobody but me would know that I had forgotten until later. (If you forget what a bid means, you cannot correct it.)

My LHO passed my 2♣ "raise" and Marty started to think. "Please don't bid too much," I silently prayed, but I didn't hold much hope. As I said before, when Marty has found a fit, he likes to bid. My "raise" had promised four diamonds, and I could see disaster looming straight ahead. "Skip bid...[1]" said Marty.

It only took a second, but it seemed like an eternity. Whatever skip bid Marty made was sure to result in disaster. "...five diamonds," he completed his skip bid.

"Double," said my RHO.

Where could I go? (Under the table was my first instinct.) I stoically passed, and tabled my dummy in 5◇ doubled. After doing so, I excused myself from the table and asked one of the kibitzers to turn the dummy. I'm not a masochist, and I saw no reason to sit around and watch Marty suffer. "I'm going to get something to drink," I said, as I left the table. Everyone probably wondered what I had already been drinking, but give me a break — haven't they ever made a mistake?

---

[1] "Skip bid" is an announcement used in duplicate bridge to warn your LHO that you are about to skip at least one level of bidding. The next player is expected to hesitate 10 seconds before making his call. Conveying information through slow passes and fast doubles, etc. must be avoided.

Several minutes later I came back, and the hand was already over. On the score sheet I saw that our result was entered as plus 750, 5◇ doubled making five! Do you believe in miracles? Check this one out:

North
♠ J973
♡ Q82
◇ —
♣ KQ9873

West
♠ AK104
♡ K10973
◇ KJ
♣ A2

East
♠ Q8652
♡ J64
◇ 1083
♣ 104

5◇ Dbl
♠A Lead

South
♠ —
♡ A5
◇ AQ976542
♣ J65

West	North	East	South
—	—	P	1◇
Dbl	2♣*	P	5◇
Dbl	All Pass		

* To err is human.

Marty ruffed the opening spade lead, and played ace and a low trump. West won, and since he could not profitably attack hearts, he played another spade. Marty ruffed and drew East's last trump. Now it was easy to knock out the ♣A, and eventually discard the ♡5 on dummy's clubs. 5◇ doubled, bid and made. Sometimes it's better to be lucky than good.

No Time to Prepare — Order Takeout

When you have a tough bidding decision, strive to be flexible. When you would like to be flexible, consider making a takeout double. When you double, you allow partner to assist in the decision-making process. When *you* do not know what to do, perhaps your *partner* will.

Do not be trapped into believing that all doubles at high levels are for penalty. In fact, level plays a secondary role in determining the meaning of a double. A good rule of thumb is: **When partner has not yet made a bid, most doubles are for takeout.**

East's intention after opening 1♡ with his strong two-suiter was to show his diamonds next — what could be more obvious?

Sometimes unforeseen developments call for a change in strategy.

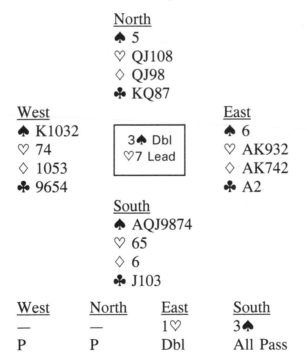

North
♠ 5
♡ QJ108
◇ QJ98
♣ KQ87

West
♠ K1032
♡ 74
◇ 1053
♣ 9654

3♠ Dbl
♡7 Lead

East
♠ 6
♡ AK932
◇ AK742
♣ A2

South
♠ AQJ9874
♡ 65
◇ 6
♣ J103

West	North	East	South
—	—	1♡	3♠
P	P	Dbl	All Pass

The vast majority of players sitting East would have bid 4◇ over 3♠ and not considered any alternative. However, East was not thrilled to be pushed to the four level by South's preempt.

East's double, even at the three level, was not for penalties and did not promise spades. In fact, it denied them. East was saying that he needed West's help in selecting the best contract. If partner responded with the expected 4♣ bid, East could still bid 4◇. Additionally, the double opened up several attractive options for West that would not have been available had East rebid 4◇.

What are those options? One is the ability to play in 3NT if West has a spade stopper and some values. Another is that the double preserves the opportunity to penalize the opponents.

And so it came to be. West was delighted to pass partner's double with his ♠K1032. It had to be easier to take five tricks on defense than winning nine or ten on offense. The 3♠ doubled contract went down two. East took four tricks, and West's trumps provided two more. Meanwhile, East-West cannot make game — no surprise given West's garbage.

If West had held a different hand, he would not have passed his partner's takeout double.

West	North	East	South
—	—	1♡	3♠
P	P	Dbl	P
???			

The flexible takeout double allows partner to handle any hand he might hold on this auction. Choose your bid with each of these hands.

♠ K54	♡ 64	◇ QJ3	♣ QJ543	3NT
♠ 975	♡ 84	◇ Q95	♣ J8764	4♣
♠ J74	♡ Q104	◇ J8	♣ Q9765	4♡

If you can do better than that, I'll buy *your* book!

An Offshape Double is Nothing But Trouble

"I had a hand yesterday that I have to ask you about," said one of my students as she arrived in class. "My opponent opened 1♥, and my hand was... Wait a minute, I wrote it down, I know you like that. I've got it here somewhere," she said, opening up a purse the size of the Grand Canyon. "Here it is."

♠ 7
♥ A64
♢ AKQ43
♣ KJ54

"Not a bad hand," I observed.

"I doubled and then..."

"Time out, Diane. How could you double 1♥ with a singleton spade?"

"I had 17 points; I was doing the big double!"

"I don't care if you were doing the twist, Diane. An overcall does not deny a good hand. You could have overcalled 2♢."

"Really! Well that's not my question. Let me tell you what happened next. It was a disaster."

"Okay, but I think we need to have a word about takeout doubles."

"Not now, Marty. I want to do this. My opponent raised to 4♥ and my partner bid 4♠."

"Your partner bid spades," said I, "what a surprise."

"Oh shush. What should I do now?"

"I don't know, did you bid 5♢?"

"Of course, but my partner thought it was a cuebid and bid 5♠! Can you believe that?"

"I've learned to believe everything, Diane. The others are here. Let's discuss takeout doubles and overcalls."

I was able to determine that the other four students would all have doubled 1♥. My gosh, it was contagious. They confirmed that they were taught that it was correct to double with any unbalanced hand containing 17 HCP. Wow, what a generalization!

♠ 4
♡ AQ865
◇ AKJ
♣ QJ65

I can't agree with a double of a 1♡ opening with this hand, not with the singleton spade. No, No, NO! I would pass.

Some hands are too strong for an overcall. If an opponent opened 1♣, you should double with:

♠ AKQJ9
♡ K10
◇ AQ96
♣ 85

Partner would pass a 1♠ overcall with the few crumbs you need. Opposite your rock-crusher, even a hand as weak as this justifies being in game:

♠ 632 ♡ Q74 ◇ K1053 ♣ 742

No one likes to double 1♣ with only two hearts. However:

1. You do have spades, the highest-ranking suit.

2. If partner jumps to 4♡ based on a lot of hearts, he will not be upset when you table this 19-count.

It is true that doubling and bidding your own suit shows a very good hand. Seventeen points is a reasonable place to initiate the big double. However, a lot of HCP does not give you *carte blanche* to double and bid your own suit.

> **The key to takeout doubles is distribution, not HCP.**

You must always look ahead and consider the consequences of your action. Isn't it ridiculous to force (beg) partner to bid his major when it is the last thing that you want him to do?

Take a look at the following hands. What is your call?

♠ —
♡ A653
◇ AKJ75
♣ AJ64

RHO opens 1♣. Never double with a void in an unbid suit. Overcall 1◇. Someone is sure to bid spades and give you a second chance.

♠ AQJ6
♡ 5
◇ A4
♣ AKQJ75

RHO opens 1◇. Double. I hope you appreciate these extraordinary cards. You probably have game in your own hand, so do not risk a simple overcall. If you overcall 2♣, you could easily miss a game.

♠ AK10965
♡ 76
◇ 7
♣ AKQ3

RHO opens 1♡. Double. It helps when your missing suit is a minor; partner is less likely to get too frisky. Also, when spades is your suit, you are in control. Although you have only 16 HCP, your chances for game are much better than with hands one (above) and four (below).

♠ AK
♡ Q
◇ AJ63
♣ K97654

RHO opens 1♠. Content yourself with a 2♣ overcall. Compare this hand with the second one above. With this hand, you have no safety at a high level. If everyone passes 2♣, you will have no regrets about playing at a lower level.

Diane and her friends are not the only ones who have been given the wrong information about doubles and overcalls. My best advice:

> **Unless you have a huge hand, do not make a takeout double with shortness in an unbid major.**

Negative Doubles: The Quintessential Convention

The negative double is the most important convention in modern bridge. The world owes its inventor, theorist Al Roth, a big debt of gratitude. Suppose you were dealt:

♠ 64
♡ AQJ6
◇ 753
♣ J1043

Your partner opens 1◇. You are ready to respond 1♡, but your RHO overcalls 1♠. Now what?

1. Can you pass? That's not very enterprising. Once partner opens, you would like to take action. It would also be nice to show your major, hoping for a fit.

2. Can you bid 1NT? No, that would show a stopper in spades, the opponent's suit.

3. Can you bid 2♣? No, you need at least 10 HCP to bid a new suit at the two level.

4. Can you bid 2◇? No, you should not support opener's minor with only three cards.

5. Can you bid 2♡? No, responder must satisfy *the requirements of five and ten* to introduce a major at the two level (five-card or longer suit and at least 10 HCP).

If you are bothered by this problem, how would you feel if your hand was better, perhaps:

♠ 7542
♡ A763
◇ Q43
♣ AQ

LHO	Partner	RHO	You
—	1◇	1♠	???

You have a strong enough hand to respond at the two level, but you do not have a suit to bid.

There is also this scenario:

♠ 63	LHO	Partner	RHO	You
♥ AKJ105	—	1◇	1♠	???
◇ 754				
♣ 983				

Once again, there is no good answer. The sad but undeniable truth is that standard bidding is sometimes very inadequate. **You need an easy, economical way to show hearts after a spade overcall.**

The solution is to redefine the meaning of double. Do not waste it in an attempt to penalize the opponents — that is silly.

You rarely hear your RHO bid spades after partner has opened the bidding and you hold:

♠ AQ1085 ♥ KJ7 ◇ 6 ♣ J873

Therefore, define the double of an overcall as a type of takeout double. It promises the unbid major with enough points (at least six or seven) to compete. Since major-suit opening bids promise five cards, responder must lead the search for the desirable 4–4 fit in an unbid major.

Responder's double after partner opens and RHO overcalls in a suit is *negative*; it is not for penalties.

With that in mind, you must also consider the following:

1.   *What suit(s) is shown by the negative double?*

Negative doubles promise length in the unbid major(s), as opposed to the minors. In an auction such as:

Opener	Overcaller	Responder
1 minor	1 major	Dbl

responder promises the unbid major, not necessarily the other minor. Here are a few of the basic applications of this convention:

Opener	RHO	Responder's Negative Double Promises
1♣	1◇	Both majors, at least 4-4.
1♣/1◇	1♡	Four spades. Bid 1♠ with five.
1♣/1◇	1♠	Four or more hearts. Responder may have five or six hearts with 6-9 HCP.
1♡	1♠	Usually both minors, because there are no unbid majors. Responder may have one minor with a weak hand.
1◇	2♣	At least one major. You are already at the two level where a new suit would promise a five-card suit and 10 HCP.

2. *How much strength does a negative double show?*

The answer is based on level. A double at the one level promises at least six or seven points, similar to what is needed to bid if RHO had not overcalled. At the two level, try to have at least eight points. Once you are at the three level, usually ten or more points are needed. Remember, you are forcing partner to bid, and he may have only a minimum opener. On the other hand, **there is no upper limit for a negative double**.

3. *Do negative doubles apply if your RHO has jumped?*

Yes, you should still use negative doubles after an opponent's jump overcall. How high? I recommend 3♠.

4. *How does opener rebid after a negative double?*

He tries to bid as if the opponent had passed. An auction that begins 1◇ – [1♠] – Dbl is similar to 1◇ – P – 1♡ and opener should rebid accordingly. After 1◇ (you) – [1♠] – Dbl* (negative) – P, what would you bid holding:

♠ AJ6 ♡ A8 ◇ KJ754 ♣ 1065	1NT
♠ 65 ♡ AQ ◇ Q10764 ♣ AQ32	2♣
♠ 76 ♡ A986 ◇ J8765 ♣ AK	2♡
♠ AQ7 ♡ QJ ◇ J8754 ♣ AKQ	2NT

5. *What should responder do when holding RHO's suit and values?*

Observe East-West in action:

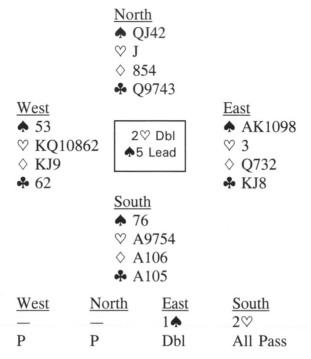

North
♠ QJ42
♡ J
♢ 854
♣ Q9743

West
♠ 53
♡ KQ10862
♢ KJ9
♣ 62

2♡ Dbl
♠5 Lead

East
♠ AK1098
♡ 3
♢ Q732
♣ KJ8

South
♠ 76
♡ A9754
♢ A106
♣ A105

West	North	East	South
—	—	1♠	2♡
P	P	Dbl	All Pass

When West overcame his surprise at the 2♡ bid, he was delighted to pass the injudicious overcall. North also passed. East was unwilling to sell out to 2♡, so he doubled. Yes, the opening bidder can make a takeout double when his partner has not bid. With shortness in the opponent's suit, opener should strive to reopen, even with a minimum.

East's double ended the auction. North-South were unhappy, while West experienced a Bergen original — EATT (Ecstasy at the Table). The 2♡ doubled contract appears to be down three or four, although the hand was never completed. West showed (he really did) declarer his trumps, and South threw his cards on the floor!

For those who are not familiar with — or are negative about — negative doubles, I am positive that they will prove invaluable to your bidding and your results.

CHAPTER 8
After the Double

Searching For Signs of Life

You are dealt the following hand:

	LHO	Partner	RHO	You
♠ KJ75	—	—	1◇	Dbl
♡ AQ74	P	1♡	P	???
◇ J3				
♣ KJ6				

I would like you to put your curiosity on hold for a few moments. Although the answer to this problem appears at the conclusion of this article, I recommend that you read all the way through so that you will understand the reasons for the answer.

Back to our hand. The key issue here is the amount of strength shown by partner's bid. It never ceases to amaze me how many experienced players believe that partner's response only addresses his choice of suit.

Here is a simple yet effective method of responding to partner's takeout double after third hand passes. Did I invent this? Absolutely not. This logical scheme is used by all the best players.

After Partner's Takeout Double
(suit responses)

1. A non-jump = 0–8 points
2. A jump bid = 9–11 points
3. A cuebid = 12+ points

All numbers include distribution

Jump shift with 9–11 points? Please, **do not think of a jump in response to a takeout double as a jump shift**. Instead, treat this jump response as a sign of life. Since you are forced to bid with nothing, it is reasonable to jump to inform partner that your hand is not in the throes of rigor mortis.

Most bridge players are guilty of being too dependent on point count. It is quite ironic that they make no effort to clarify their point count here.

LHO	Partner	RHO	You
1◇	Dbl	P	???

♠ 104
♡ 9863
◇ 9762
♣ 753

♠ Q93
♡ KJ1093
◇ 762
♣ 52

Bid 1♡ with both of these hands. With the hand on the right, you will compete to 2♡ if necessary.

♠ 94
♡ KJ108
◇ 7542
♣ AQ9

Jump to 2♡, invitational. Partner will pass with a minimum double. Can you jump in a four-card suit? Absolutely! Partner did promise support for all the unbid suits, especially the majors.

♠ Q2
♡ K832
◇ A1072
♣ A92

Cuebid 2◇. You are on your way to 4♡ if partner has four hearts; otherwise you will play 3NT. The cuebid is not game forcing, but you must drive to game with this nice hand.

When would you respond 1NT? Not very often. Partner's double asks you to select an unbid suit. However, with 5–10 points, no major, and a good holding in the opponent's suit, it is the indicated action.

LHO	Partner	RHO	You
1◇	Dbl	P	???

♠ Q32
♡ J5
◇ KJ94
♣ 9742

Respond 1NT. Do not even think about passing.

♠ A6
♡ 962
◇ A9742
♣ 942

If you lack values, stay out of notrump.

♠ Q1097
♡ 64
◇ 764
♣ 9743

LHO	Partner	RHO	You
1♠	Dbl	P	???

Respond 2♣. Otherwise you will find yourself in 3NT doubled when partner has a big hand.

What would you bid with the following hands after partner doubles the opponent's opening preempt?

♠ AQ754
♡ K104
◇ 74
♣ 853

LHO	Partner	RHO	You
3♣	Dbl	P	???

Jump to 4♠.

♠ 63
♡ K3
◇ A98
♣ Q97642

LHO	Partner	RHO	You
3♠	Dbl	P	???

Jump to 5♣. You are fortunate to hold a six-card suit and three useful cards. You would be forced to bid 4♣ with: ♠ xx ♡ xxx ◇ xxxx ♣ xxxx.

When you are forced to bid, nobody will be impressed just because you honor your obligation. Imagine the following divine plan for the distribution of high cards:

1. Every player begins bridge life with the same quota of good cards.

2. A record is kept of the way each player invests these values.

3. Honors and more honors will be bestowed upon those players who divulge their assets. As for those spoiled Scrooges who fail to appreciate the bounty they have been given — bah humbug! They will be condemned to receive Yarboroughs (hand with no card above a nine) until they repent.

Answer to the question that began this chapter

	LHO	Partner	RHO	You
♠ KJ75	—	—	1◇	Dbl
♡ AQ74	P	1♡	P	???
◇ J3				
♣ KJ6				

You know partner has 0–8 points, so there is no future in this hand. Not only should you not jump, you should not bid anything. Pass, and hope partner can take seven tricks. If he has a terrible hand, you may already be too high.

The Goal After Redouble is to Kick Butt!

"The penalty double is an integral part of the game. Without it, there would be no way of preventing rambunctious souls from bidding forever."

Anonymous

After partner's opening bid has been doubled, a redouble promises at least 10 points. Most players do not realize what that really means. Although your side has the clear balance of power, the opponents have decided to enter the bidding. However, they have yet to find a fit; in fact, they may not have one. Even if they are able to locate their best suit, they may lack the firepower to make anything.

What should opener's side do after redoubling? Try for penalties, go for blood! Average players consider only their own cards; experienced players love to pounce on the opponents when they step out of line.

The stage is set for a lucrative penalty double. Opener should go for the jugular with four trumps. At the two level, he can even double with three good trumps. The redoubler will overrule the suggestion with a singleton. Otherwise, he will be delighted to cooperate with opener in teaching the opponents an expensive lesson.

If unable to double, opener will bid only if he has something worth saying. He will strain to pass the auction back around to his partner, hoping that he will be able to double. The redoubler will be delighted to do so with adequate trumps; otherwise he will bid.

If they have a fit, you do, too. Once you establish that your side has the balance of power, the only time the opponents can end up declaring is when you choose to *hit them* (bridge slang for a penalty double).

For example, you deal as South and pick up:

	West	North	East	South
♠ AQ754	—	—	—	1♠
♡ 76	Dbl	Rdbl	2♣	???
♢ AJ53				
♣ J6				

Do not bid 2♢. What's your hurry? Maybe partner can double 2♣. Pass and give him a chance.

Should opener ever bid in the auction above? Absolutely, with a hand that screams for offense.

West	North	East	South
—	P	P	1♠
Dbl	Rdbl	2♣	???

♠ KQJ976
♡ KQ10
♢ 6532
♣ —

You would rebid 2♠ with this hand. Allowing the opponents to play in a suit contract when you have no trumps is offensive in and of itself.

♠ Q8754
♡ 54
♢ AKQJ7
♣ 8

With this hand, you would make the obvious 2♢ bid; now you have a suit that you are eager to show.

Observe how East-West handled matters on this hand:

North
♠ KQ
♡ QJ107
♢ J76
♣ KQJ7

West
♠ A9754
♡ AK4
♢ 5432
♣ 5

2♢ Dbl
♡A Lead

East
♠ 103
♡ 8652
♢ AK
♣ A10642

South
♠ J862
♡ 93
♢ Q1098
♣ 983

West	North	East	South
1♠	Dbl	Rdbl	2♢
Dbl	All Pass		

West was delighted to double 2♢ with four trumps, three quick tricks (♠A and ♡AK) and a singleton club. Some would question the quality of West's diamonds, but remember, length is more important than strength.

West led the ♡A then shifted to his singleton club. It was easy for the defenders to take eight tricks; the obvious six aces and kings plus two club ruffs. Declarer was down three, doubled and vulnerable — good for a juicy 800 points! It is worth noting that East-West had no game, no surprise given their 22 HCP and misfitting hands. If West had not doubled, his side would have ended up with a minus score. East would have bid 2NT and played there, with no chance of taking eight tricks. Very often, the best offense is a good defense.

"Do You Know?" (From *The Complete Book of Takeout Doubles* by Michael Lawrence)

Every one of the following statements refers to the same well-known convention. Can you identify it?

1. It is the oldest in use today.

2. It is the most misunderstood.

3. It has no upper limit regarding strength.

4. It is the one that is used most often.

5. It is not a bid.

6. Partner must respond without any points.

What is this well-known convention? The takeout double.

How Do I Support Thee? Let Me Count the Ways

"Points, schmoints! Support with support."

Marty Bergen

Do you know the meaning of 1♡ – Dbl – <u>3♡</u>? Everyone agrees that the bid promises good trump support. However, many players believe responder is inviting game — that 3♡ shows a limit (invitational) raise with 10–12 distribution points. no, No, NO, that is not correct!

When you first learned about takeout doubles, you were taught that you must redouble whenever you have 10 or more points.

<table>
<tr>
<td>

♠ A2
♡ 864
◇ K754
♣ K863

</td>
<td>

♠ A8532
♡ KJ4
◇ Q3
♣ 1085

</td>
<td>

After your partner's 1♡ opening is doubled, it is *incorrect* to bid 3♡ with either of these hands. The proper action is to redouble, then support hearts.

</td>
</tr>
</table>

After a double, responder's jump raise shows four trumps and less (usually much less) than a limit raise. This weak jump raise is based on The Law of Total Tricks. Partner opened 1♡, so you know he has at least five hearts. When you have four, the partnership has nine (or more). According to The Law, you should always compete to the three level with nine trumps. Can you live with that? Trust me, The Law is smarter than any player in the world.

After the auction begins 1♡ – Dbl, jump to 3♡ with:

<table>
<tr>
<td>

♠ 64
♡ K1084
◇ 87632
♣ 53

</td>
<td>

The 3♡ bid is a *weak jump raise*. Why should you jump preemptively? You would like to prevent the opponents from finding their fit. If you do not bid now, the opponents will have free rein to get to their optimum spot, and you have no defense. Your hand is worthless unless hearts are trump.

</td>
</tr>
</table>

```
♠ 2
♡ 108653
◇ A642
♣ 954
```

Do not bid 3♡ with this hand. You have five trumps. Your partnership has 10 hearts. Bid 4♡.

Should you make the same bids vulnerable? Only if you like to win.

The concept of the weak jump raise also works when partner opens one of a minor. With a weak hand and five-card support for partner's minor, you make the jump raise. Yes, five-card support is enough if partner opens 1♣ or 1◇ — he probably has a four-card suit.

```
♠ 54
♡ 76
◇ 9754
♣ KQ965
```

```
♠ 6
♡ 96
◇ 108543
♣ QJ1087
```

RHO doubles partner's 1♣ bid.

In both cases your bid is 3♣.

```
♠ A4
♡ 876
◇ J9654
♣ 754
```

```
♠ 4
♡ 962
◇ K8643
♣ 9642
```

RHO doubles partner's 1◇ bid.

Bid 3◇ with both hands.

It should come as no surprise that *weak jump raises* occur frequently after RHO's takeout double. By virtue of his double, RHO has announced that he is short in opener's suit. Someone has length there and if it is you, bid to the level of The Law.

It is important to show support for partner via this weak jump raise. It is also worthwhile to notice the effect your bid has on LHO. You have deprived him of two levels of bidding, which he may have needed to define his strength and locate a fit.

Now you know what to do with support for partner and a weak hand. Sometimes you will be dealt support and a good hand.

♠ A85
♡ J1054
◇ Q3
♣ K1085

Partner opens 1♡ and RHO doubles. What action should you take?

Perhaps you would redouble. This will inform partner about your strength, but he would have no idea about your great support. You would prefer to find a way to say it all in one bid.

Good news, help is on the way — courtesy of Alan Truscott, bridge editor of *The New York Times*. With redouble available to show 10 or more HCP, Alan appreciated that responder's jump to 2NT (showing 13–15 HCP) was redundant. Therefore, he redefined the bid as showing **10 or more distributional points with four-card trump support.** This convention is called *Jordan 2NT. Voilà.*

Watch *Jordan 2NT* in action. Partner opens 1♠ and RHO doubles:

♠ AJ105
♡ K7
◇ J9764
♣ 107

Bid 2NT. This is a classic limit raise. Do not worry if you fail to make 3♠. The opponents must be cold for 3♣ or 3♡ (so says The Law). You are much too strong for a 2♠ or 3♠ bid.

Your partner opens 1♣ and RHO doubles:

♠ 65
♡ 87
◇ AK72
♣ QJ974

Bid 2NT. Jordan can also be used after minor-suit openings. Try to have five trumps in order to justify bidding at the three level (The Law).

You are now armed and ready to support when partner has opened the bidding. *Weak jump raises*, *The Law* and *Jordan 2NT* have bolstered your bidding arsenal. That will teach the opponents to double you!

CHAPTER 9
Competitive Bidding — Like Four People Boxing

Overcalls: If the Suit Fits, Bid It

> *"More points are lost at the bridge table through bad or pointless overcalls than any other way."*
>
> *Helen Sobel Smith*

One of the most important tools of competitive bidding is the overcall. Unfortunately, a great deal of confusion surrounds this subject.

The purpose of overcalling is to inform partner about a good, long suit. Overcalls serve to get your side into the auction, suggest a specific lead to partner, and take away bidding space from the opponents.

Notice that I said nothing about HCP. This omission was deliberate. In many situations, points are secondary: They are not the basis for an overcall. After a 1♣ opening bid, you should overcall 1♡ with both:

♠ 10864	♠ 6	**An overcall neither promises**
♡ AQJ106	♡ A8642	**nor denies an opening bid.** If
◇ 643	◇ AKQ	that does not set you straight on
♣ 8	♣ KJ75	the subject of HCP, nothing will.

Let's deal with a few basic issues.

1. *If your HCP total is not the key factor in overcalling, what is?*

   A. Level

   At the one level, almost anything goes, especially nonvulnerable. It is safe to bid at this level; someone is likely to rescue you if you are in the wrong contract.

   The criteria for two-level overcalls are significantly different; still, points are not crucial. It is far more difficult for everyone to bid at this level. You need a better suit since you must be concerned about getting stuck in your bid, possibly even doubled.

B. Suit quality

The strength of your suit is often critical. This is especially true when overcalling at or above the two level. Only be lax about suit quality when overcalling at the one level. Here is a guideline:

Suit length	One-level overcall
5 cards	Have at least two honors or a strong hand.
6 cards	Suit can be very weak.

Suit length	Two-level overcall
5 cards	Avoid mediocre five-card suits. The suit should be headed by at least three honors.
6 cards	Suit may be weak when nonvulnerable. Unless your hand is very strong, have at least two honors when vulnerable.

C. Vulnerability

Vulnerability is of minor importance at the one level, but better players are careful with their vulnerable overcalls at higher levels.

D. Your Holding In Opponent's Suit

Try to be aggressive when you have shortness in the opponent's suit, but conservative with length. This is true regardless of whether RHO opens at the one level or preempts.

An essential key of competitive bidding:
**The hand with shortness in the opponents'
suit must strive to take action.**

---

2. *Let's look at some acceptable one-level overcalls.*

Your RHO opens 1♢:

♠ AKJ95   ♡ 865   ♢ 7   ♣ 8654

Bid 1♠ because of your great spade suit and diamond singleton.

♠ A6 ♡ 87643 ◇ 84 ♣ AKJ9

Bid 1♡. Despite the horrible heart suit, you must overcall at the one level with this good hand. You should *never* overcall with five small cards at the two level.

♠ KJ764 ♡ Q7 ◇ 852 ♣ K85

With this mediocre hand, bid 1♠ only if nonvulnerable.

3. *Overcalling at the two level.*

A. Overcall 2◇ over 1♠ with each of the next three hands. Notice that the suit is either very strong or at least six cards long. Also, the minimum strength is greater than it was at the one level.

♠ K97 ♡ 7 ◇ AQ10943 ♣ 985

The suit is strong, and I love that singleton.

♠ 92 ♡ 86 ◇ KQJ106 ♣ AJ75

Some players would choose to pass if vulnerable. The lead-directing advantage if on defense is too important to pass up.

♠ 9 ♡ A96 ◇ Q97643 ♣ AJ5

A weak six-card suit is acceptable with a reasonable hand. The singleton in RHO's suit makes this a no-brainer.

B. Do not overcall 2◇ after an opening bid of 1♡ with each of the next two hands, at any vulnerability.

♠ A86 ♡ J5 ◇ AJ754 ♣ A54

Double. Don't bid 2◇ with this nice hand, indifferent five-card suit, and acceptable support for the unbid suits.

♠ Q7 ♡ QJ76 ◇ K8654 ♣ KQ

Pass. All you have is a pile of junk. You have length and strength in hearts and five lousy diamonds. You would have opened 1◇ but that is irrelevant. Overcalling and opening are not the same.

C. With these strong hands, there is no alternative to a 2♦ overcall after a 1♡ opening:

♠ 6 ♡ A532 ♦ AKJ75 ♣ AJ6

♠ AQ ♡ 86 ♦ AQ9654 ♣ K86

4. *Some hands are too strong for an overcall.*

Yes, but not as many as most players believe. In order to initiate the *big double*, you must be prepared to handle likely follow-ups, and believe that you could miss game if your overcall is passed out. Notice my failure to mention HCP. "When in doubt, bid your suit."

These examples will clarify your action with very good hands after an opponent's opening bid of 1♣:

♠ 8 ♡ AK7 ♦ AKQ8765 ♣ 54

Bid 1♦. Someone will find a spade bid at this low level. Do not make takeout doubles with shortness in an unbid major.

♠ A75 ♡ KQJ974 ♦ AK4 ♣ 8

Double. What could possibly go wrong? You are prepared for every contingency and would miss game by overcalling 1♡ if partner held:

♠ K3 ♡ 652 ♦ 8652 ♣ 9643

5. *What about overcalling after both opponents have bid?*

You must exercise greater care in *the sandwich seat*. The sandwich overcall is so named because the bid is made between two bidding opponents. If you have a good hand, partner must be weak. How many players can have good hands on one deal?

After 1♦ – P – 1♠ – ???

♠ AJ54 ♡ A7 ♦ Q9 ♣ K8643

pass, Pass, PASS. If you overcall at the two level with this moth-eaten suit, you are asking for trouble.

♠ 1096 ♡ A7 ♦ 53 ♣ KQJ1053

Bid 2♣. Now there's a club suit worth bidding.

6. *Is it ever correct to overcall in a four-card suit?*

Yes. For instance, RHO opens 1♦ and you hold:

♠ 6 ♡ AKQ10 ♦ 8754 ♣ A865

You must not double with a singleton spade. Anyone who doubles 1♦ holding only one spade should be boiled in oil, but why waste good oil? You hate to pass with your nice hand, but sometimes you are stuck for a bid. Fortunately, there is an easy solution.

If I asked 100 of the world's best players (who have not agreed on anything in years) what they would do here, all 100 would bid 1♡. They would even ask, "What's the problem?" At the one level, it is considered routine to overcall with strong four-card suits.

However, do not get carried away with your new toy. Partner is expecting a five-card suit and will support you with three small. A four-card overcall should contain three honors. If vulnerable, the hand should resemble an opening bid. An overcall based on a four card suit is recommended only when you have no reasonable alternative.

After an opponent's 1♦ opening bid, what would you bid with:

♠ AKQ3 ♡ 87 ♦ KQ2 ♣ Q865	Overcall 1NT.
♠ AJ5 ♡ AK102 ♦ 653 ♣ Q98	Double.
♠ 64 ♡ AK73 ♦ QJ96 ♣ 865	Pass.
♠ KQJ9 ♡ 86 ♦ A108 ♣ K865	Bid 1♠.

Armed with a formidable array of weapons, you are now prepared to seize any opening (bid) you might encounter.

Stand Tall After a 1NT Overcall

Bridge is easy to play but difficult to play well. Compare it with another tough, frustrating game — golf. There you can see the results of your actions immediately. Even a novice knows that driving, chipping and putting involve different techniques. In both games, each new situation demands a different strategy.

However, bridge is far more subtle. Partner opens 1◇ and you have the following hand. You are waiting for your opponent's call, and though you may not realize it, you are totally dependent on his action.

	Action by RHO	Your response
♠ 743	Pass	1♡
♡ Q954	Double	Redouble
◇ Q7	1♡	1NT
♣ KQJ10	1♠	Double (negative)
	2♣	Pass (hoping that partner reopens with a double)

Very interesting. Your response varies, depending on RHO's call. Who would have thought such a thing?

Compare the situations above to those in which you might find yourself after hitting your tee shot on a short par three.

Result of tee shot	Your response
Land in a sand trap	"Darn," sand wedge.
Land in water	"Oh shoot," new ball. Don't forget to add a penalty stroke.
On the fringe	"Why me? Sure hope I hit a good chip."
On the green	"Yessss! Jeeves, I will take the putter."
In the hole	"Drinks for everyone; why weren't there more spectators?"

Back to bridge. There is yet another action by RHO that you must be prepared to handle, one that many players fail to consider.

What would you do if RHO had overcalled 1NT, promising the values to open 1NT with at least one diamond stopper? (Notrump overcalls always promise stoppers in the opponent's suit; it is foolish to be unprepared after being warned.)

Let me help you out. Can your opponents make 1NT when you have 10 points and partner has opened? No way. Dummy must be broke! Give partner 12 HCP, you have 10, and the overcaller has about 16. That totals 38, which leaves *bubkes* for the dummy.

If you choose to defend, you will enjoy odds of two-against-one. In addition, your side has the advantage of the opening lead.

LHO	Partner	RHO	You
—	1◇	1NT	???

♠ 742
♡ Q954
◇ Q7
♣ KQJ10

The only correct action is to double for penalty. (Negative doubles apply only after an overcall in a suit.) A nice bonus is that you have the tailor-made opening lead of the ♣K.

How much do you need to double when partner opens and RHO bids 1NT? Nine HCP will suffice. Your double announces that you believe your side has the balance of power.

If responder should double with all hands containing 9 HCP, it follows that **any other bid made by responder** *denies* **strength** — another example of "*Points, schmoints.*" Support partner with support, following The Law. If you do bid a new suit, it must be a worthwhile one; after all, partner has not promised any support.

As a matter of fact, **after a 1NT overcall, even jump bids deny strength**. What a concept! You do not necessarily need more to bid more — what you *do* need is a great fit or a long suit.

What would you do with each of these hands?

	LHO	Partner	RHO	You
	—	1♡	1NT	???

♠ Q987642
♡ 9
◇ 865
♣ 98

Bid 2♠. You didn't expect me to pass a seven-card suit, did you?

♠ 9765
♡ 8
◇ KQ10875
♣ 65

Bid 2◇. This diamond suit deserves a mention. Sometimes, minor suits play a major role.

♠ J7543
♡ A7
◇ 9654
♣ J6

Pass. The spade suit leaves a lot to be desired.

♠ 86
♡ QJ107
◇ 85
♣ 96542

Bid 3♡. Wheeee! The Law of Total Tricks in action. A perfect weak jump raise.

♠ K87
♡ J105
◇ A964
♣ K43

Double. You have them exactly where you want them. If they make 1NT doubled after the ♡J lead, I will eat the cards.

Do You Know Your Balancing Basics?

"Bridge is a 52-card game. This simple statement is overlooked by many bridge players. All too often the bridge player thinks of the game as a 13-card game — the hand he holds."

Ira Corn, founder of the Dallas Aces

What goes through your mind on an auction such as:

West	North	East	South
—	—	1♡	P
2♡	P	P	???

If it is, "Thank goodness, the opponents didn't bid game, what should I lead?" have I got a tip for you.

Here is what passes through my mind. "My opponents are attempting to steal the bid at a low level. Partner must have some strength. They have a fit, so we must have a fit. I am certainly not going to roll over and play dead. What action should I take?"

Balancing is a difficult concept to master. It can be defined as reopening the bidding after the opponents' auction has died at a low level. A player is in the *balancing seat* when his pass would end the auction. In contrast, a player is in the *direct seat* when his RHO took action. In many low-level auctions, you must not allow the opponents to steal the bid.

After [1♡] – P – P, you should bid 1♠ with this weak hand:

♠ KJ1086
♡ 7
◇ K854
♣ 954

Why is that?

You are certainly not happy about defending 1♡ with this hand. The opponents only need seven tricks and you would be painfully short of trumps if you passed.

Partner must have a very good hand. Responder, by virtue of his pass, has fewer than six points. Suppose he has a three-count. You have 7 HCP, leaving 30 (40 minus 10) between partner and opener. Even if opener had as many as 16 HCP, partner would be marked with 14. Why didn't he act with his good hand?

Partner is stuck for a bid with either hand after his RHO opens 1♡. He must pass.

Can you appreciate partner's problem? Even with good hands, there may be no alternative to passing. Since partner must pass with hands like these, you should strain to balance with shortness in the opponent's suit.

There are many advantages to balancing:

1. Your bid may push the opponents one trick too high.

2. Instead of watching them make their cozy partscore, you may make one of your own.

3. If your side defends, your bid may help partner select a good lead as well as give him a better picture of your hand.

4. When partner has a very good hand, you may bid game or give him the opportunity to penalize the opponents.

Now that you see the need for balancing, I would like to address how to balance. The following may be new to you. In addition, you may not like hearing it. However, let it be known:

> **Actions in the balancing seat differ from those in the direct seat.**

Overcalls in the Balancing Seat

Even at the two level, a balancing overcall might be made with as few as 7–8 HCP.

LHO	Partner	RHO	You
1♠	P	P	???

♠ 43
♡ K94
◇ AJ8763
♣ 85

♠ 8
♡ 1073
◇ KJ9875
♣ K102

Bid 2◇, although you are too weak to have taken this action in direct seat.

Since you may have a weak hand, partner must tread lightly. He will content himself with an invitational 2NT holding a good hand like:

♠ AQ5   ♡ AK65   ◇ 42   ♣ 9763

After [1♠] – P – P, you would also bid 2◇ with this strong hand:

♠ 43
♡ 82
◇ AKQJ6
♣ A842

It is difficult to calculate game possibilities after a balance because so little is known about fourth-hand's strength. However, no one has come up with a better solution. This is one of the many reasons to open the bidding whenever possible.

Balancing Jump Overcalls

Since fourth hand can balance with a modest hand, he needs a way to show strength. A jump bid promises solid values.

♠ AQJ763
♡ 4
◇ 754
♣ A73

♠ AJ9853
♡ K7
◇ AJ10
♣ 63

LHO opens 1♣, which is passed around to you. Jump to 2♠ with each of these hands.

Are you thinking, "I use weak jump overcalls, so 2♠ should show a weak hand?" I use weak jump overcalls also, but only in the direct seat.

LHO	Partner	RHO	You
1 Y*	P	P	???

* Y could be any suit.

Once your RHO denies six points, why bother to preempt? **In the balancing seat, a jump overcall shows an intermediate hand — an opening bid and a good six-card suit.** This is a little-known fact. Indeed, a jump to the three level would show hands as strong as:

LHO opens 1♠ followed by two passes. Bid 3◇ with the first hand, 3♡ with the second hand.

♠ A43
♡ 62
◇ AKQJ54
♣ 95

♠ 76
♡ AKJ643
◇ AK3
♣ 72

1NT in Balancing Seat

If you are eager to balance in fourth seat, you will not want to pass out 1♡ with hands like these.

You cannot double because you have only two spades. Bid 1NT with both hands.

♠ K4
♡ AJ5
◇ K875
♣ J743

♠ A5
♡ J84
◇ Q1075
♣ AQ93

A balancing 1NT overcall does not promise an opening 1NT bid. As you can see, it can even be bid without a stopper in the opponent's suit. Remember, life is different in the balancing seat; it's now or never. Your 1NT bid shows about 11–15 HCP here. With more, you would double first, then bid notrump.

2NT in Balancing Seat

A jump to 2NT after two passes should not be treated as the *unusual notrump*, emphasizing the two lower unbid suits. The 2NT bidder needs roughly 19–21 points. However, the hand may not be balanced. If partner has some values, he can raise. After:

LHO	Partner	RHO	You
1♡	P	P	???

Bid 2NT with both hands.

| ♠ AQJ |
| ♡ KQ6 |
| ◇ Q4 |
| ♣ AQ943 |

| ♠ A |
| ♡ AQ6 |
| ◇ KQ854 |
| ♣ KJ65 |

Double in Balancing Seat

A balancing double is for takeout, and asks partner to bid. As with most balancing seat actions, less strength is required.

LHO	Partner	RHO	You
1♡	P	P	???

Double with both hands. In direct seat, you would be too weak to take action.

| ♠ K865 |
| ♡ 64 |
| ◇ A1085 |
| ♣ QJ7 |

| ♠ AJ94 |
| ♡ 8 |
| ◇ Q9653 |
| ♣ Q98 |

A balancing double does not deny a good hand.

♠ KQ32	LHO	Partner	RHO	You
♡ 8	1♡	P	P	???
◇ AQJ2				
♣ AJ86				

Double. What's the problem? With this nice hand, you have only just begun.

Every aspiring bridge player needs to understand the concept of balancing. The following auction screams for a balance.

LHO	Partner	RHO	You
—	—	1Y*	P
2Y*	P	P	???

* Y could be any suit.

With the right shape, I also love to balance after:

LHO	Partner	RHO	You
1NT	P	P	???

and

Preempt	P	P	???

Nobody can master everything about balancing in one lesson. However, if you are...

1. Determined to be competitive;

2. Willing to listen to the bidding; and

3. Able to think about what the other players hold,

... you could be surprised with your results and the respect that you generate. You just might overhear your opponents say: "{*Your name here*} has become so tough to play against. I never do well against him/her anymore. What does he/she know that I don't?" *All about balancing!*

CHAPTER 10
Preempts For Fun and Profit

Sock It To 'Em With an Opening Three-Bid

What do you need for a three-level preempt?

1. You should have less than an opening bid, including distribution. The following hand is too strong. Open 1♠, based on the Rule of 20.

    ♠ AQ86532 ♡ 5 ◇ KJ4 ♣ 64

2. An opening three-bid should contain fewer than 10 HCP. The exact number is not important.

3. Suit quality is crucial. The difference between preempting with QJ76432 (versus QJ109853) can be one or two tricks. A suit with good texture is a big plus.

    However, do not open at the three level with a suit headed by the AKQ. A solid seven-card suit is too good. Open 1♣ with:

    ♠ 6 ♡ 53 ◇ J72 ♣ AKQ10865

4. Vulnerability is definitely relevant, as it is with all preempts and overcalls. Avoid making a vulnerable preempt with a weak suit like K976432. However, do not worry when your suit is good. Too many otherwise sensible players forget to make the indicated bid *because they were vulnerable!* If you fail to open 3♡ with the following hand, I would rather be your opponent than your partner:

    ♠ 5 ♡ KQJ10986 ◇ 954 ♣ 86

5. Distribution is also important. 7-3-3-0 is better than 7-3-2-1, which is better than 7-2-2-2.

6. Avoid preempting with too many outside honors. Even though I love to preempt, I would not open 3◇ with this mess:

    ♠ KJ10 ♡ Q6 ◇ J876532 ♣ Q

7. Three–level openings ususally promise a seven-card suit. The only exception would be 3♣, when you may have only six clubs because 2♣ is not available as a preempt. Be happy to open 3♣ with:

   ♠ 9 ♡ 74 ◊ 10762 ♣ KQJ1097

8. The above applies when preempting in first or second seat. *In third seat*, you should try harder to preempt. Your LHO must have a good hand. Make him sweat. Open 3♠ with:

   ♠ KQJ987 ♡ — ◊ 10986 ♣ 643

   Open 3◊ with:

   ♠ 2 ♡ K6 ◊ AQJ9765 ♣ J106

9. *In fourth seat*, there is no reason to preempt with a weak hand. Pass and take your chances on the next deal if you hold:

   ♠ 97 ♡ KQJ8754 ◊ 75 ♣ J6

   In fourth seat, only open three with a promising hand. After three passes, open 3♠ holding:

   ♠ AKQJ1074 ♡ 7 ◊ 532 ♣ 43

   The philosophy of third and fourth-seat preempts also applies to weak two-bids. In third seat anything goes. Fourth-seat bids are not *weak*; 9–12 HCP is a reasonable range.

10. Last, but certainly not least, be attuned to partner's style. Knowing whether partner is aggressive, conservative, or middle-of-the-road is critical. I believe that knowing partner's tendencies is as essential as remembering the conventions you have agreed to play.

   For the remainder of this section, assume neither side is vulnerable. Partner is a sensible, middle-of-the-road type.

Responding to Preempts is a Cinch

What should you do after partner opens three of a major? This question is a lot easier to answer than most players realize, because:

1. You know a great deal about what partner has — a weak hand with a good seven-card suit. He is interested in playing only in his major. You can almost **see his hand** before you see his hand.

2. Unless you have a fantastically strong hand or an unbelievable suit of your own, there are only two realistic options. Most of the time you pass; sometimes you raise partner's major to game.

Since responses to 3♡ and 3♠ openings are almost identical, we will use 3♠ for the purposes of our discussion.

First, let's dispose of those hands you will probably never hold. If partner opens 3♠:

Bid 4♡. You will take more tricks in a heart contract than in spades.

Bid 4NT. Sign off in 5♠ if partner has no aces. Opposite the expected one ace, you will bid 6NT. It would be very unlucky if the opponents could obtain a ruff in 6♠, but why take the chance? If partner shows two aces after his preempt, you will quickly recover from the shock and bid 7NT.

Bid 3NT. Partner can never correct, regardless of his hand. Do not be embarrassed if you bid diamonds, many players would have done the same. However, once you think of it, 3NT should be a snap. For 3NT to be defeated: West (you are South) would have to lead a spade; then, if partner does not have the ♠A, East would have to win the first trick and find the club shift; West would need to hold the ♣A; and partner must have no club help whatsoever. At this point you would have to be considered the world's unluckiest human being on your worst day. My advice is to immediately leave the game; hire a bodyguard; hire a driver after carefully checking references; go home; lock all the doors and windows; hope and expect that tomorrow will be a better day (because it surely can't get any worse).

So much for hands you will never hold. Over partner's 3♠ bid, what do you do with:

♠ Q
♡ AQ64
◇ K53
♣ QJ643

You have 14 HCP, but that is irrelevant. Partner has less than an opening bid, so you do not have enough for game. Anyone who believes that, "When partner preempts, you must respond holding an opening bid," should discard that falsehood ASAP. Pass.

♠ —
♡ KQJ5
◇ KQ732
♣ KQ85

Pass! Many players would bid 3NT but there is no way to win nine tricks opposite partner's weak spade-oriented hand. What good will his spades be in notrump when you have no entries to his hand? **Remember: There is a lot more to a successful no-trump contract than having all suits stopped**.

♠ 5
♡ KJ7
◇ AKJ9876
♣ 98

Pass again. Your suit is better than partner's, but where are you going? You are probably already too high. Sometimes, silence is golden.

Responder has an easy raise to game when he has support for partner and great playing strength. Here are some examples:

♠ K86
♡ AK82
◇ AQ43
♣ 75

♠ QJ
♡ A965
◇ A865
♣ KQJ

Raise 3♠ to four with each of these hands.

With very strong hands, despite meager support, you should still raise partner to game.

♠ K
♡ AK74
◇ KQ53
♣ A854

If you would have bid 3NT before reading this, I believe you. However, consider what partner's hand looks like:

♠ AJ109842 ♡ 62 ◇ 84 ♣ 96.

You tell me, would you rather play 3NT or 4♠?

♠ 3
♡ KQ85
◇ AK72
♣ AK32

4♠ again. Have you gotten the message? When a player opens with a three-level preempt in a major, he is interested only in playing the hand in his suit.

You may be wondering about bidding 3NT. That would be a shutout bid; opener is supposed to pass. In all the years I have been playing bridge, I have never responded 3NT to partner's opening 3♡ or 3♠ bid. Does that give you an idea of how rarely the perfect hand comes along?

```
♠ —
♡ AK65
◇ A9753
♣ AKJ2
```

If you answer this correctly, go to the head of the class. Raising with a void may go against all your instincts, but try to picture partner's hand. With spades as trump, partner has five or six tricks which combine nicely with your five. 3NT looks hopeless because dummy's spades would be inaccessible.

You may also extend partner's preempt based on the premise, *support with support*. Partner opens 3♠ and RHO passes. You hold:

```
♠ Q85
♡ 63
◇ A954
♣ 7542
```

Most players would pass — you probably will not even make 3♠. However, you are dreaming if you expect the opponents to sell out to 3♠ when they are short in spades and have 26 HCP. They must be cold for 4♡. After your ◇A and a possible spade trick, what are you going to do for an encore?

Perhaps you are thinking that you can wait until the opponents bid 4♡ and then sacrifice in 4♠. If so, your sense of timing is way off. Passing 3♠ will give the opponents room to exchange information about their hands. In addition, the delayed sacrifice will make it obvious that you have a weak hand.

The answer is to bid 4♠ immediately. This greatly clouds the issue for the enemy. They will not know whether you are sacrificing or your bid is based on strength.

Is there an easy way to know that you should raise 3♠ to 4♠? There certainly is — apply The Law. Partner has seven spades and you have three. Your 10 trumps allow you to compete to the four level with impunity. Do not worry about HCP. *Points, schmoints!*

This technique is called an *advance sacrifice*. It is the most effective type of sacrifice, because it is made before the opponents have a chance to exchange information and find their best contract.

What could be easier? You may not play like an expert, but when you know how many trumps partner has, you and The Law constitute a formidable partnership.

"Getting it off Her Chest" (Adapted from *Have I Got a Story for You*)

A husband and wife (we'll refer to them as Mr. and Mrs. Bridge) were losing heavily at rubber bridge. Finally they decided that the only way to recoup their losses was to cheat.

"Darling," Mr. Bridge counseled, "if you want me to bid diamonds, just point to your ring finger. You get the idea."

The very next time they sat down to play, Mrs. Bridge's RHO preempted with a 3♠ bid. Mrs. Bridge casually put her hand on her chest and passed. LHO also passed, and Mr. Bridge confidently bid 4♡. He was doubled and went down 1100 points.

When they got in the car for the ride home, Mr. Bridge exclaimed to his spouse, "What were you thinking? You had no points and only one heart. How could you tell me to bid them?"

Taken aback, Mrs. Bridge exclaimed: "Oh my, is that what you were thinking? I was trying to tell you I had a bust."

The Weakest Weak Two-Bid Ever Made

"Desperate situations often warrant desperate measures."

Anonymous

I agree! Such was my analysis late in the finals of the 1983 Spingold Teams, a major event that can lead to the world championships. Time was running out. Our team was trailing by a significant margin.

| ♠ 87642 |
| ♡ J93 |
| ◇ AK3 |
| ♣ 104 |

As dealer, vulnerable, I held the East cards. Although I had the most routine pass you could imagine, I found something to say. I had a fancy bid available, and I could not afford to wait around for the perfect hand. I therefore opened 2◇, which, in our system, promised a weak two-bid in spades.

Do not worry about this unusual convention — this is a story, not serious bridge advice. If you are thinking that anyone who preempts with 87642 is not of sound mind, I agree. I could say that I had missorted my hand, and my spades were really AK8764, but that would be a fib. To tell the truth, I was desperate. How did this ridiculous action turn out? It exceeded my wildest dreams.

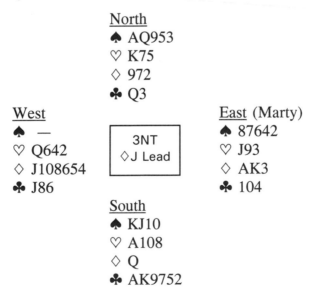

North
♠ AQ953
♡ K75
◇ 972
♣ Q3

West
♠ —
♡ Q642
◇ J108654
♣ J86

3NT
◇J Lead

East (Marty)
♠ 87642
♡ J93
◇ AK3
♣ 104

South
♠ KJ10
♡ A108
◇ Q
♣ AK9752

West	North	East	South
—	—	2◇*	2NT
P	3NT	All Pass	

* A weak two-bid in spades!

If you would have overcalled 3♣ with South's hand, I understand. However, many experts would bid 2NT. With the required stoppers in the opponent's suit, they do not lose sleep about the others. Even if South had overcalled 3♣, North would have bid 3NT like a shot. As long as North-South had spades stopped and no heart fit, 3NT was inevitable.

If you are interested in the identity of North and South, they are two of the best players in the world. South was Bobby Wolff, many-time national and world champion. North was his longtime partner, Bob Hamman, who is considered by many to be the world's best player.

Against 3NT, my partner, Larry Cohen, cleverly avoided a spade lead. He led the ◇J, which I won with the king. South's queen was a beautiful sight. I cashed the ◇A and we ran diamonds for down two.

In what contract would you like to play with the North-South cards? The correct answer is 6♠. Despite the terrible trump split, East's spades are only a minor annoyance. Declarer will draw trumps and run clubs, losing only one diamond trick.

I had opened a weak two-bid in a suit in which my opponents could make a slam. This must qualify as another world record. Some players collect trophies, some collect world championships. I seem to specialize in obscure records.

Did this wonderful result help us win the Spingold? Alas, it did not. Our teammates reached 6♣, which failed on a spade ruff (the ◇A providing the second trick). Down one meant that our gain on the hand was minimal. We had our fun, but it was all for naught.

The moral of this story: If thou art desperate, thou wilt probably lose. Does anyone know where I can trade several obscure records for one world championship?

Why Not Have a Grand Old Time

You are pleased to be dealt a terrific hand:

```
♠ KQJ103
♡ AQ5
◇ AK743
♣ —
```

Your side is vulnerable. Before you have a chance to open 2♣ (strong, artificial and forcing), partner opens 2♡, a weak two-bid. Your RHO passes, and the spotlight turns to you. How will you proceed?

Partner's weak two-bid shows a good six-card suit with little, if any, outside strength. The normal range is 5–10 HCP. It also makes a strong statement about his choice of trump suit.

However, **the key to preempts is suit strength, not points**. Vulnerability is also relevant. Let's clarify with some examples. As dealer, do you preempt or pass with these three hands?

```
♠ KQJ1065
♡ 54
◇ 1075
♣ 92
```

With this magnificent suit, a weak 2♠ bid is correct at any vulnerability.

```
♠ 84
♡ J5
◇ A107432
♣ Q62
```

This hand contains more HCP than the previous one, however I would open 2◇ only if nonvulnerable. Purists would never even dream of preempting with such a mediocre suit.

```
┌─────────────────┐
│ ♠ Q76532        │
│ ♡ QJ            │
│ ◇ KJ            │
│ ♣ J87           │
└─────────────────┘
```

Pass. This is neither a two bid nor a one bid. I love to bid, but there is simply no justification with this mess. You have a horrible suit, as well as a lot of scattered strength.

Let us return to our actual hand. Partner opened 2♡.

```
┌─────────────────┐
│ ♠ KQJ103        │
│ ♡ AQ5           │
│ ◇ AK743         │
│ ♣ —             │
└─────────────────┘
```

You can place partner with six hearts headed by the missing KJ10 for his vulnerable preempt. Can you appreciate that slam is justified, even if partner has nothing else?

You will obviously not lose any club tricks — that's a great start. The hearts are solid, no losers there. You expect to lose one spade trick to the ace. Partner might worry about a diamond loser if he has three small cards in that suit, but that is not realistic. He will discard his diamond loser on your spade winners once he knocks out the ♠A.

A direct 6♡ bid is not bad. Certainly, it is better than bidding 4♡, and that answer does get some votes. However, even 6♡ does not get you an A+ in my class.

If partner holds the ♠A, you will not have any losers. Fortunately, it is easy to discover if partner has that important card.

To discover more about the weak two-bidder's hand, responder bids 2NT. The 2NT bid is artificial; it does not suggest a notrump contract. It asks opener: "Do you have a minimum weak two-bid?" If he does, opener will rebid three of his suit. With more, he bids a suit in which he has a feature (ace or king).

With your hand, you are fantasizing that opener can bid 3♠, showing the ♠A (since you hold the king). If he does, you can jump confidently to 7♡, which must be cold. If partner bids anything else, you will have to content yourself with a small slam. Are you ready for the full deal?

North
♠ KQJ103
♡ AQ5
◇ AK743
♣ —

West
♠ 972
♡ 84
◇ Q6
♣ A109653

```
┌─────────┐
│   7♡    │
│ ♣A Lead │
└─────────┘
```

East
♠ 654
♡ 63
◇ J1085
♣ KQ82

South
♠ A8
♡ KJ10972
◇ 92
♣ J74

West	North	East	South
—	—	P	2♡
P	2NT*	P	3♠**
P	7♡	All Pass	

  *   Artificial and forcing.
  ** Shows a non-minimum hand with a spade feature.

As expected, there was nothing to the play. Declarer ruffed the opening lead and drew trump. No muss, no fuss.

The weak two-bid — one of the best of the modern conventions. Isn't it wonderful to be able to play out the hand during the auction?

CHAPTER 11
The Rule of 11: Can You Subtract?

Partner Leads Fourth Best — What Next?

Use The Rule of 11 to determine your play:

> **When a fourth-best lead is made, subtract the card led from 11. The difference represents the number of higher cards held by the other three players (excluding the opening leader).**

Do not lose sleep figuring out why this works; just accept it. The following is also worth knowing about The Rule of 11:

1. It does not apply when an honor card is led.

2. Contrary to popular opinion, The Rule of 11 *does* apply in suit contracts, provided the lead is fourth-best.

3. The higher the card led, the easier it is for third hand to learn more about declarer's holding by applying The Rule of 11.

You are East, after North raised South's 1NT opening bid to 3NT.

North
♠ K53
♡ QJ9
◇ Q32
♣ K543

East (You)
♠ AJ92
♡ A643
◇ J98
♣ J7

| | | 3NT | |
| | | ♠7 Lead | |

West	North	East	South
—	P	P	1NT
P	3NT	All Pass	

For those who prefer to see all 52 cards, the complete hand is at the top of the next page.

West leads the ♠7. Here are the spades in view:

>   North
>   ♠ K53
>   West   East (You)
>   ♠ 7   ♠ AJ92

The ♠3 is played from the dummy. Which card would you play? Stop now and make your decision before reading on.

Your thinking should be: 11−7=4, which means there are a total of four cards above the 7 between declarer, dummy, and you. You have three: the ace, jack and nine. Dummy has one higher card, the king. Therefore, declarer has no card above the seven! Isn't that interesting?

It is easy for your side to win this trick, but your objective is to run spades. The ♠A is an absurd play; clearly, the opponents do not deserve to win their king. You could win the trick by playing the nine or the jack, but what would you do for an encore? A spade continuation would allow dummy to win the king and limits your side to three spade tricks. It is difficult to imagine any other tricks for your side besides the ♡A.

If you believe that your partner is going to obtain the lead later in the hand, do not hold your breath. Dummy has 11 points, you have 11, and your partner has the ♠Q, for a total of 24. Whether your opponents open 1NT with 15–17 or 16–18 points, partner has nothing else.

The only correct play is the ♠2, allowing partner to hold the first trick. (So much for always playing third-hand high. This is one of a million exceptions.) When West recovers from the shock of winning the trick with the ♠7, he will continue the suit. It will then be child's play for East-West to win four spade tricks plus the ♡A.

You should not be concerned that West might shift after seeing you play the deuce. West should reason: "If I just won the trick with my seven, partner must have some great spades." Therefore, West should be delighted to lead another spade.

Here is the entire layout:

North
♠ K53
♡ QJ9
◇ Q32
♣ K543

West
♠ Q1087
♡ 52
◇ 764
♣ 10862

3NT
♠7 Lead

East (You)
♠ AJ92
♡ A643
◇ J98
♣ J7

South
♠ 64
♡ K1087
◇ AK105
♣ AQ9

One more for the road. Again, you are East, defending 3NT. Your partner leads the ♡5 against the same 1NT – 3NT auction.

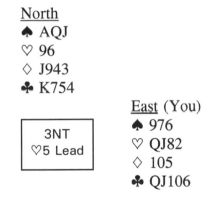

North
♠ AQJ
♡ 96
◇ J943
♣ K754

3NT
♡5 Lead

East (You)
♠ 976
♡ QJ82
◇ 105
♣ QJ106

Twice in a row, partner found your length and strength. Way to go! The ♡6 is played from dummy and you play the jack, cheapest of equals. Declarer takes the trick with his king and continues with the ace, king, and a small diamond. Partner wins the third round with the queen, and the time has come for you to discard. What is your choice?

Sometimes bridge hands yield absolute answers, and sometimes they do not. On this hand, there is only one correct discard, the ♡Q!

The Rule of 11 told you that declarer had one heart above the five-spot. There are six higher cards outstanding (11–5), and five of them are held by you and dummy. Declarer must have exactly one card above the five — the king, which he played at trick one. *You* know that all of partner's hearts are winners, so tell him loud and clear.

If you are wondering why this spectacular discard is necessary, here is the entire deal:

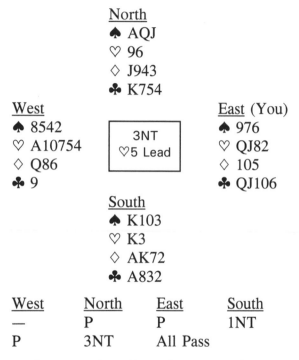

North
♠ AQJ
♡ 96
◇ J943
♣ K754

West
♠ 8542
♡ A10754
◇ Q86
♣ 9

```
3NT
♡5 Lead
```

East (You)
♠ 976
♡ QJ82
◇ 105
♣ QJ106

South
♠ K103
♡ K3
◇ AK72
♣ A832

West	North	East	South
—	P	P	1NT
P	3NT	All Pass	

If you make any other discard, can you be sure partner will lead a second heart? Without the ♡Q discard, West might picture declarer with an original heart holding of KQx. South would then be left with Qx after trick one. West would attempt to find an entry to your hand, playing you for either the ♣A or ♠K, so that you could lead a heart through South. You know that West should lead more hearts. Do not make him guess.

The Rule of 11 is indispensable to the defenders. Unfortunately, this information is public property. When declarer is alert, he will sometimes enjoy the last laugh.

Declarer Passes the Test

After a fourth-best lead is made, declarer's first thought should be to apply The Rule of 11. This is easier to focus on in notrump, where spot-card leads are always fourth-best. In a suit contract, The Rule of 11 will still be meaningful after a fourth-best lead. However, declarer must proceed with caution; against suit contracts, the opening lead will often be made from a shorter suit.

The following hand illustrates declarer's use of The Rule of 11. After receiving the ♣6 lead, what card would you play from dummy?

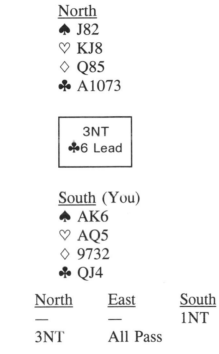

North
♠ J82
♡ KJ8
◇ Q85
♣ A1073

3NT
♣6 Lead

South (You)
♠ AK6
♡ AQ5
◇ 9732
♣ QJ4

West	North	East	South
—	—	—	1NT
P	3NT	All Pass	

Did you figure out that East has no club above the six? 11−6=5. Declarer and dummy have five clubs greater than the six; thus, East cannot possibly beat dummy's ♣7.

You must win the first trick with the ♣7, saving your honors for later. Now it is easy to enter the South hand in hearts and finesse clubs. Eventually you will win four club tricks, regardless of when West plays his king. Along with two spades and three hearts, you will have four club tricks, and your contract is in the bag.

If you carelessly played the ♣3 from dummy at the first trick, you would have to waste an honor from your hand to win the trick. The club position would be:

North
♣ A107

West   East
♣ K982   ♣ —

South
♣ Q4

Unfortunately, there is no longer any hope for a fourth club trick as long as West is awake. He will be happy to cover if the queen is led. If declarer leads the four, West will insert the eight or nine.

For those who believe that they would have found a way to make 3NT after playing dummy's ♣3 at trick one, here's the entire deal:

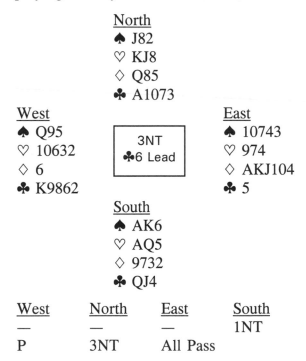

North
♠ J82
♡ KJ8
♢ Q85
♣ A1073

West
♠ Q95
♡ 10632
♢ 6
♣ K9862

3NT
♣6 Lead

East
♠ 10743
♡ 974
♢ AKJ104
♣ 5

South
♠ AK6
♡ AQ5
♢ 9732
♣ QJ4

West	North	East	South
—	—	—	1NT
P	3NT	All Pass	

If you can take nine tricks after playing the ♣3 at trick one (assuming correct defense), feel free to call me — collect.

CHAPTER 12
Don't Be Stumped When Playing Notrump

Not a Good Declarer, But What a Great Dummy

One hand I will never forget took place in a tournament in 1978. I was giving a playing lesson to a pleasant gentleman from Philadelphia, whom I had just met.

After George turned ten tricks into eight in 3NT, I knew that declarer play was not his strong suit. I got into the swing of things, determined to make George the dummy whenever possible. Then came board 19.

North
♠ A105
♡ A108532
◇ KQ10
♣ 3

West
♠ KJ4
♡ K97
◇ 732
♣ AJ42

East
♠ 983
♡ Q
◇ 654
♣ Q98765

```
3NT
♣2 Lead
```

South (Marty)
♠ Q762
♡ J64
◇ AJ98
♣ K10

West	North	East	South
—	—	P	1◇
P	1♡	P	1NT!
P	3♡	P	3NT!
P	P!	P	

The bidding — especially mine — was *interesting*. Why did I open the bidding with that garbage? When playing with a conservative partner, I find it essential to get in ASAP. I should have bid 1♠ over 1♡, going up the line in case partner held four spades. However, I was in a big hurry to grab the notrump.

George should have bid 4♡ over 1NT. He knew that we had the values for game, and I needed two or three hearts for my notrump rebid. Perhaps he just wanted to allow me to declare 3NT.

Great minds think alike — I bid 3NT. George would declare a heart contract; I would declare notrump. Case closed.

(Deal repeated for convenience)

North
♠ A105
♡ A108532
◇ KQ10
♣ 3

West
♠ KJ4
♡ K97
◇ 732
♣ AJ42

| 3NT |
| ♣2 Lead |

East
♠ 983
♡ Q
◇ 654
♣ Q98765

South (Marty)
♠ Q762
♡ J64
◇ AJ98
♣ K10

West	North	East	South
—	—	P	1◇
P	1♡	P	1NT!
P	3♡	P	3NT!
P	P!	P	

I cursed myself after seeing dummy; 3NT had no chance with the club lead. I won East's ♣Q with my king, but now what? I had to lose at least one heart trick, and the opponents would then run clubs. The ♣2 lead suggested that clubs were dividing 4-6, so it appeared that 3NT would be down two; at best I would lose one heart and five club tricks.

Was there any hope for the 3NT contract? I did see a long shot, based on the average player's tendency to "cover an honor with an honor." I led the ♡J, dreaming that West would cover and East had been dealt a singleton heart honor.

As luck would have it, all this came to pass. When both heart honors hit the table on the same trick, the opponents looked like they had just been notified of an IRS audit. I was now assured of twelve tricks: the ♣K, six hearts, four diamonds, and the ♠A. Making 3NT with three overtricks was a great result, but I was not through. I was now ready to apply Bergen's Law #43: Where there are 12 tricks, there may be 13.

After winning the ♡A, I overtook the ◇K to return to my hand. I led the ♡4 and topped West's seven with dummy's eight. I now ran hearts from the top as the opponents grudgingly discarded. Having a great time, I cashed the ◇Q, and led the ten to my jack. Here was the position as I led my ◇9 at trick 11:

North
♠ A105
♡ —
◇ —
♣ —

West
♠ KJ
♡ —
◇ —
♣ A

East
♠ 9
♡ —
◇ —
♣ 98

South
♠ Q
♡ —
◇ 9
♣ 10

To add insult to injury, West was squeezed. He correctly discarded the ♣A in the hope that his partner had been dealt the 10. No dice. I cashed my ♣10 and made seven.

The atmosphere at the table was... *interesting*. West appeared ready to strangle himself, with East quite willing to furnish the rope. As for George, his naiveté and innocence provided the perfect contrast. "Sorry Marty, I had a feeling that we had a slam!"

Are You Guilty of Premature Grabbing?

"It is not the handling of difficult hands that makes the winning player. There aren't enough of them. It is the ability to avoid messing up the easy ones."

S. J. Simon, British bridge writer

Many players' natural instinct is to rush to win any tricks they can. This is not the way to go. How often have you witnessed an inexperienced declarer in 3NT win the first seven tricks and...lose the remainder? He never had a plan of attack; he just grabbed everything in sight.

Only *grab* when you are in a position to fulfill your contract or defeat the opponents. Rather than playing trick by trick, learn to consider the big picture. Be patient.

An expert's first move will often result in losing a trick; in fact, he may lose several. However, once his plan is under way he cruises along smoothly, and the next thing you know, he has nine tricks in the bank. **Lose your losers early** is often excellent advice.

On this deal, declarer was favored with a helpful opening lead:

```
                    North
                    ♠ 654
                    ♥ J743
                    ◇ KQ54
                    ♣ 104
    West            ┌──────────┐      East
    ♠ AK1032        │   1NT    │      ♠ J9
    ♥ Q852          │ ♠3 Lead  │      ♥ 106
    ◇ 9             └──────────┘      ◇ J1083
    ♣ 962                             ♣ AK873
                    South
                    ♠ Q87
                    ♥ AK9
                    ◇ A762
                    ♣ QJ5
```

West	North	East	South
—	P	P	1NT
All Pass			

Declarer was delighted to win his ♠Q after East played the ♠J at trick one. Declarer was no beginner; he knew that West had no more than five spades after the lead of the three. (When a player leads fourth-best, he always has three higher cards. With the lead of the three, there is at most one lower card. Therefore, West's maximum length was five cards.) Declarer also knew that it is *usually* correct to attack his longest suit in notrump. Unfortunately, all this knowledge was not sufficient to allow this confirmed grabber to "see the forest for the trees."

South had six obvious tricks: two hearts, three diamonds and one spade. After counting his winners, he turned his attention to his eight-card diamond fit. He realized that a normal 3–2 division of the outstanding diamonds would provide a seventh trick. Unfortunately, after grabbing the ◇AK, the bad split rendered the diamond length useless.

Declarer next turned his attention to hearts, his second-longest suit. He cashed the ace and king, noting the appearance of East's 10. Declarer had won the first five tricks when he led the ♡9 to West's queen, setting up dummy's jack. He hoped that the ◇Q and ♡J would see him home.

However, it was too late. West ran spades, while East encouraged in clubs. The defense was now able to take four spade tricks, one heart and two clubs for down one.

Declarer erred at trick two. With dummy's lovely ♣10 solidifying South's ♣QJ5, developing one club winner was a sure thing. If declarer had attacked clubs immediately, the defenders could never have taken more than two clubs and four spade tricks.

Many players merrily take their sure winners, hoping that something good will happen. If you are content to play like the Joneses (no offense intended), you can continue to grab. However, if you want more (tricks) out of life, I suggest that you keep in mind: "Anybody can grab aces and kings; good players create something out of nothing."

If You Don't Have Entries, You Ain't Got Nothing

"Failing to prepare is preparing to fail."

Vince Lombardi, legendary football coach

Declarer must exercise great care with his entries. This is especially true in notrump contracts where the source of tricks can sometimes be found in the weak hand.

> **Declarer must insure that at least one entry remains in the weak hand until its long suit is ready to run.**

Unfortunately, key plays are not always obvious. At that special moment, it would be nice if:

1.   A bell would go off;

2.   Someone would stand up and yell "alert";

3.   A little bird would whisper "now" in your ear;

4.   A guardian angel would protect you from yourself.

No such luck, you are on your own. It is time for you to demonstrate your prowess. ***Big hint***: The first trick is often the most important.

```
                        North
                        ♠ KJ9
                        ♡ A8654
                        ◇ A4
                        ♣ AK4
         West                           East
         ♠ 107643      ┌─────────┐      ♠ Q85
         ♡ Q2          │   3NT   │      ♡ KJ93
         ◇ 8653        │ ♠4 Lead │      ◇ K7
         ♣ J5          └─────────┘      ♣ Q1087
                        South
                        ♠ A2
                        ♡ 107
                        ◇ QJ1092
                        ♣ 9632
```

West	North	East	South
—	1♡	P	1NT
P	3NT	All Pass	

Consider your strategy before reading on, just as you would when actually playing. When dummy comes down, take some time to plan the play of the hand. Try to think beyond the first trick. This applies whether you are declaring or defending, and will definitely improve your results.

Declarer needs to establish diamonds to make his contract, but his one outside entry is the ♠A. The only way to ensure that it won't be removed prematurely is by rising with dummy's king at trick one. Declarer now turns his attention to diamonds by playing ace and another. This illustrates an important principle: **When working on your long, strong suit, use up (unblock) the honor(s) from the short side first.**

Two key plays: ♠K, ♢A, and nine tricks are in the bag.

A Record That Will Never Be Broken

"Some men see things that are and say why, I see things that never were and say why not."

Robert Kennedy

All sports and games have their records, some of which may never be broken. Because of one hand, I hold a unique record — one that I'm 100% positive will never be broken.

While playing in a national tournament several years ago, I was North on the following deal:

North (Marty)
♠ KJ1094
♡ J1098
◇ Q
♣ KJ6

West		East
♠ 7		♠ A863
♡ A32	3NT	♡ K765
◇ 8742	♡2 Lead	◇ 103
♣ A9732		♣ 1054

South
♠ Q52
♡ Q4
◇ AKJ965
♣ Q8

West	North	East	South
P	P	P	1NT*
P	2♣	P	2◇
P	3NT*	All Pass	

* Imaginative.

I passed in second seat, and my partner opened 1NT (15–17). I responded 2♣, Stayman, asking about the majors. Partner denied a four-card major by bidding 2◇.

With my aceless hand, it did not seem right to try for 10 tricks. I was concerned that we might have a lot of fast losers; so I chose to suppress my five-card spade suit and jumped to 3NT.

West's opening lead of the ♡2 was strange. I would have led the ♣3 without a second thought, delighted to be holding a five-card suit and two entries. What did West have in mind? I can only believe that he was overreacting to the following: **When selecting an unbid suit to lead against notrump, prefer a major.**

Anyway, on to the play. East chose to withhold his king at trick one; instead; he signaled encouragement with the seven. After winning the first trick in dummy, declarer led the ♠J, which held. East also ducked the ♠10, but took his ace on the third round when the king was led.

East returned his partner's heart lead, and the defense took their ace and king. East now shifted to the ♢10, which was won in dummy with the queen. Declarer led a club to the queen and West's ace.

Here was the position with West to lead at trick nine. Declarer needed the rest of the tricks to make the contract.

```
                      North
                      ♠ 94
                      ♡ J
                      ♢ —
                      ♣ KJ
     West                              East
     ♠ —                               ♠ 8
     ♡ —                               ♡ 6
     ♢ 87                              ♢ 3
     ♣ 973                             ♣ 105
                      South
                      ♠ —
                      ♡ —
                      ♢ AKJ96
                      ♣ —
```

Obviously, the contract was not in jeopardy; both the North and South hands contained nothing but winners. However, there was a great deal at stake for me. I concentrated fiercely and West obliged by leading a club rather than a diamond.

Why did it matter? Reporting this hand in *The New York Times* on July 29, 1992, Alan Truscott wrote: "The diagramed deal from the first hand of the Spingold Knockout Teams set an unobtrusive world record. It was so unobtrusive that the declarer did not realize it, and it can be predicted that few readers will spot the unusual feature of the deal."

Do you see what happened? The North hand, although unable to open the bidding, won all nine tricks! After opening 1NT, declarer failed to take a single trick in *his hand* in a contract that succeeded.

I do not know what fate has in store for me, but of one thing I am sure. On a lovely summer day in Toronto, Marty Bergen was the only passed-hand dummy in the history of bridge to single-handedly fulfill a game contract.

Nothing Obscure About These Guys

1. What actor has been seen playing bridge in an old, frayed raincoat?

2. What two famous non-American leaders played bridge early in the 20th century? (Hint: Their initials are W.C. and M.G.)

3. What foreign actor prefers bridge to acting, horses and women?

4. This president was described by Oswald Jacoby as "in general, a superior bridge player."

Answers:

1. Columbo (Peter Falk)

2. Winston Churchill, Mahatma Gandhi

3. Omar Sharif

4. Dwight D. Eisenhower

CHAPTER 13
Some Players Do it With Finesse

Hold That Finesse

> *"A finesse is a tool; and you don't use a tool without rhyme or reason, just because it happens to be lying about."*
>
> *Alfred Sheinwold*

Do you like to finesse? Would you believe I do not?

I will never forget my initial exposure to finesses. I was 14, and my mother had just given me my first bridge book, the best-selling *5 Weeks to Winning Bridge* by Alfred Sheinwold. After 18 chapters of basics and bidding, I could not wait to play. Chapters 19 and 20 dealt with finessing. As I read, I practiced with a deck of cards. It was going well, and I could not wait to play so that I could finesse until I dropped...

Chapter 21 was titled "When Not to Finesse!" Wow! Sheinwold began by stating: "Having learned how to finesse, we must now decide whether to do so." You could have knocked me over with a feather. He gave many examples of hands where it was wrong to finesse. Incredible.

Of course, the above is inevitable. In any game, the first step for new players is to learn the basics. Once they understand them, the next step is to apply that knowledge.

When it comes to finesses, a major philosophical difference separates the masses from the most accomplished players. Most players are eager to finesse. Finessing is simple and can provide immediate gratification. **Experts do not like to finesse**, and never have. Why? Finesses lose half the time. I compare the expert's mindset with that of a professional gambler: Do you think he gets rich on 50–50 propositions?

Now, try to make this slam without relying on the club finesse.

```
                      North
                      ♠ 54
                      ♡ QJ104
                      ◇ 872
                      ♣ J985
West                ┌──────────┐      East
♠ 97632             │   6♡     │      ♠ J108
♡ 8                 │ ◇K Lead  │      ♡ 73
◇ KQ103             └──────────┘      ◇ 9654
♣ K73                                 ♣ 10642
                      South
                      ♠ AKQ
                      ♡ AK9652
                      ◇ AJ
                      ♣ AQ
```

West	North	East	South
—	—	P	2♣*
P	2◇**	P	2♡
P	4♡	P	6♡

All Pass

*   Strong, artificial and forcing.
** The recommended, artificial response,
     allowing opener to describe his hand.

After the ◇K lead, declarer is faced with two possible losers, a diamond and a club. Many players can't wait to take the club finesse after drawing trumps. The chances of success are 50–50. You deserve better. (*Hint*: Keep in mind that West's opening lead marks him with the ◇Q.)

Win the first diamond, and play the ♡Q and ♡J. Cash your spades, discarding a diamond from dummy. Here is the layout at trick seven:

North
♠ —
♡ 104
◇ 8
♣ J985

West
♠ 9
♡ —
◇ Q103
♣ K73

East
♠ —
♡ —
◇ 965
♣ 10642

South
♠ —
♡ AK96
◇ J
♣ AQ

Now throw West in by leading the ◇J from your hand. After winning the ◇Q, he is endplayed. A spade or diamond lead allows you to ruff in dummy and sluff the ♣Q from your hand. After West's club lead, you know what to do when playing last with the AQ.

An endplay can be an invaluable aid in avoiding finesses. Suppose you have a side suit consisting of:

North
♡ AJ6

South
♡ K104

If you are going to tackle this suit, you must attempt to guess which opponent holds the queen. Notice what happens if the opponents can be forced to lead hearts. Now, you are assured of three winners by playing second hand low, based on the sound principle of *last is best*.

Try one more for the road. Any declarer can make 4♠ here if he is lucky enough to find East with the ◇K. Can you succeed as is? *Marty's cryptic hint*: *Many people would be willing to relinquish one diamond if they could be assured of never losing their heart.*

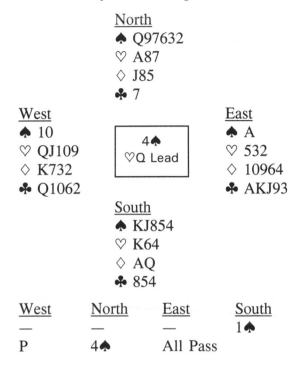

North
♠ Q97632
♡ A87
◇ J85
♣ 7

West
♠ 10
♡ QJ109
◇ K732
♣ Q1062

4♠
♡Q Lead

East
♠ A
♡ 532
◇ 10964
♣ AKJ93

South
♠ KJ854
♡ K64
◇ AQ
♣ 854

West	North	East	South
—	—	—	1♠
P	4♠	All Pass	

Declarer is concerned about losing four tricks, one in each suit. It may appear that a diamond finesse is the best hope, but what's your hurry? Take another look at that handsome jack in the dummy. Win the ♡K at trick one, preserving dummy's ♡A entry.

Next, you must unblock the ◇A. At trick three, lead the ◇Q, sacrificing her majesty in order to set up dummy's ◇J. West can win the ◇K and return a heart, which is as good as anything. You win *on the board* with the ♡A , and cash the ◇J, discarding your last heart. Your only remaining losers are the two black aces.

Regarding finesses: Know how to execute them, but think twice before taking them.

Take Everything in Sight

Play

Given the ability to see all 13 cards, and no shortage of entries to each hand, can you win three tricks against perfect defense? The lead is in the South hand.

North
A92

West   East
K5   J1076

South (You)
Q84<u>3</u>

Lead low from the South hand and insert the nine when West plays low. East will win the 10. When you regain the lead, cash dummy's ace, capturing West's king. It is now easy to lead dummy's two and finesse through East's remaining J7 — you have the Q8 behind him. For those interested in bridge lingo, this is an example of an *intra-finesse*.

Defend

You are East defending a notrump contract. From the previous play, it is clear you need to attack this suit. Can you win four tricks here?

North
1076

West   East (You)
A93   K<u>J</u>82

South
Q54

The answer is to lead the jack, which serves to neutralize dummy's ten. If South ducks, your jack holds. Your side then wins the ace and king, ending in your hand with the good eight.

Suppose South covers the jack with his queen. West wins his ace and returns the nine. Now you are sitting pretty with the K82 behind dummy's 107. This *surrounding play* allows you to run the suit. Well done!

I Never Met a Five-Card Suit I Didn't Like

The average declarer's point of view is often short-sighted. All he notices are his honor cards. He begins the play of a hand by grabbing the obvious winners, then tries a finesse or two. When the smoke clears, all he has won is what he had coming — no more, no less.

The expert has a totally different perspective. He is able to win tricks with small cards that his less experienced counterparts never noticed. He appreciates long suits and their ability to produce extra tricks. Any schmoe can win tricks with aces and kings; the expert finds it aesthetically more pleasing to win tricks with twos and threes.

On the following deal, nobody would be impressed with the quality of dummy's diamonds. Fortunately, declarer was not a nobody; he knew that length is usually more important than strength. His persistence in attacking diamonds paid off; he succeeded in bringing home 10 tricks without taking a heart finesse.

North
♠ K10
♡ AQ4
◇ 65432
♣ K65

West
♠ 753
♡ J95
◇ AQ8
♣ QJ109

```
      4♠
    ♣Q Lead
```

East
♠ 92
♡ K1072
◇ K1097
♣ 874

South
♠ AQJ864
♡ 863
◇ J
♣ A32

West	North	East	South
—	1◇	P	1♠
P	1NT	P	4♠
All Pass			

South saw the possibility of four losers: one club, one diamond and two heart tricks if East held the king. By playing diamonds at every opportunity, declarer demonstrated how good players generate winners in their long suits.

Declarer proceeded in the hope that the opponents' seven diamonds were divided 4–3. If they were not, there would still be time later to take the heart finesse.

South won the opening club lead in his hand because it was crucial to preserve entries to dummy. At trick two he led the ◇J. West won his queen and continued the club attack; no other play would affect the outcome. After winning the ♣K, South ruffed a diamond, leaving the opponents with a total of three cards in that suit.

Declarer played a spade to dummy's 10 — *good card, partner!* He then ruffed another diamond with a high trump. When everyone followed, he knew that diamonds were dividing 4–3. A spade was led to dummy's king, and the normal 3–2 trump split was noted. It was now easy to trump dummy's fourth diamond, felling East's king, and pull the last trump.

Declarer could not risk the heart finesse because he was out of trumps (three diamond ruffs, three rounds of trump). With dummy's ♡A and ◇6 delivering tricks nine and ten, South was delighted to score up his game.

Finesses Do Have Their Day in the Sun

Although forgoing a finesse is often the correct play, there are times when a finesse is necessary:

1. When there is no alternative;

2. When the finesse is *odds on* based on the bidding or early play;

3. When the finesse offers the best chance to develop the key suit.

On this deal, declarer needed to find a ninth trick in 3NT.

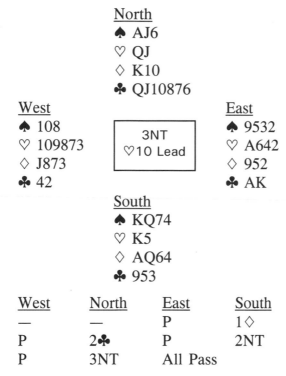

North
♠ AJ6
♡ QJ
◇ K10
♣ QJ10876

West
♠ 108
♡ 109873
◇ J873
♣ 42

East
♠ 9532
♡ A642
◇ 952
♣ AK

3NT
♡10 Lead

South
♠ KQ74
♡ K5
◇ AQ64
♣ 953

West	North	East	South
—	—	P	1◇
P	2♣	P	2NT
P	3NT	All Pass	

West led the top of his sequence against the unlucky 3NT contract. (Note that dummy's heart honors were no more useful than the three and two would have been!) East won his ace and returned a heart, and after the second trick, everyone knew that South could not afford to lose the lead. Declarer could count only eight winners: four spade tricks, three diamonds and one heart. There was no time to develop dummy's clubs; South had no hope of surviving the inevitable *heart attack*.

Was this contract doomed by the opening lead?

Not necessarily. Declarer had a legitimate 50% chance. If West held the ◇J, a finesse would provide a fourth diamond trick. At trick three, declarer led the ◇4 and held his breath as he finessed dummy's 10. When this won, he was home.

He continued with the ◇K, then unblocked the ♠AJ, using up the honors from the short hand first. It was now easy to play a spade to his hand, where a plethora of winners awaited him.

In addition to the obvious eight winners, declarer had scored his ninth trick with the aid of the subtle diamond finesse.

Here is another example of a subtle finesse. North is on lead.

North
Q74

South (You)
A105

South needs to win two tricks in this suit to fulfill his contract. He should not lead the queen — he cannot afford to sacrifice that card. A useful rule of thumb for declarer is: **Lead an honor for a finesse only when you hope to see it covered.** If your reaction after the honor is covered is "*darn*," you should not have led it in the first place.

Begin by crossing to the South hand in a side suit and lead the five. If West has the king, you are home free. If he takes it, the queen becomes a winner. If West ducks, the queen will win the trick.

However, if West plays low and dummy's queen is captured by East's king, do not give up. Enter the North hand in another suit and lead the four toward your ten. As long as East holds the jack, your second trick is in the bag.

In the following 4♠ contract, declarer saw five possible losers: three club tricks, one diamond, and one heart:

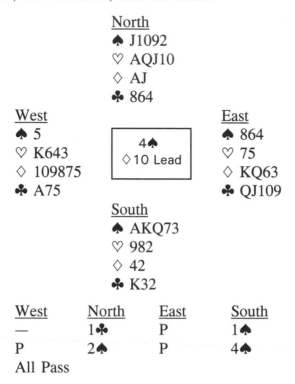

North
♠ J1092
♡ AQJ10
◇ AJ
♣ 864

West
♠ 5
♡ K643
◇ 109875
♣ A75

4♠
◇ 10 Lead

East
♠ 864
♡ 75
◇ KQ63
♣ QJ109

South
♠ AKQ73
♡ 982
◇ 42
♣ K32

West	North	East	South
—	1♣	P	1♠
P	2♠	P	4♠
All Pass			

Declarer's goal is to win four heart tricks whenever West holds the ♡K. This could require three finesses. Fortunately, the AKQ of trumps provide the necessary entries. Declarer hopes to discard a minor-suit loser on the fourth heart.

Declarer won the diamond lead and cashed the ♠J. He continued with a second trump and won in hand with the ace. Ignoring East's last trump, declarer began finessing hearts. When the ♡Q won, it was easy to return to the South hand with the ♠K to repeat the finesse. Dummy's last spade was led to the carefully preserved ♠Q to take another winning finesse. The ♡A was now available to discard a minor-suit loser, allowing South to survive the fact that the ♣A was offside.

Declarer demonstrated good technique with his careful play. Drawing three rounds of trumps immediately would have wasted a vital entry to South's hand. A successful finesse is a big help, but timing is everything.

How Low Can You Go?

"One advantage of bad bidding is that you get practice at playing atrocious contracts."

Alfred Sheinwold

Everybody knows how to finesse with AQ opposite 43. But that is just the tip of the iceberg. It is possible to finesse against virtually any card.

I am sure that you bid far too well to arrive at a contract that requires the desperate measures needed on the following hand. However, in case the same cannot be said of your partner, I would like to present — the *ultimate finesse*:

North
♠ 1092
♡ KQJ
♢ KQJ5
♣ A65

```
6NT
♡10 Lead
```

South
♠ AK64
♡ A73
♢ A86
♣ J43

West	North	East	South
—	—	P	1NT
P	6NT	All Pass	

West leads the ♡10 against the overambitious 6NT contract. An invitational 4NT bid (not Blackwood) would have been a better call with the North hand. Be that as it may, you are now in a slam with only 10 winners: two spades, three hearts, four diamonds and one club. Your only hope of making the contract is to win two extra spade tricks.

Believe it or not, there is a solution! Your only hope is that the opponents' cards are arranged in the following manner:

North
♠ 1092

West
♠ 87

East
♠ QJ53

South
♠ AK64

You lead the 10 from dummy and East covers with the jack; it would not help him to duck. You win with the king, as West drops the seven. You now cross back to dummy and lead the ♠9, which East covers with the queen. (Once again, you would be okay if East ducked.) You capture this with your ace, felling West's eight.

You have succeeded in setting up your six as a third winner, but you still require an additional trick. Here is the remaining layout:

North
♠ 2

West
♠ —

East
♠ 53

South
♠ 64

Return to dummy and lead the ♠2. When East plays the three, you finesse your four. This represents a successful finesse against the five. You now cash your six and chalk up your slam. *Well bid, partner*! Isn't bridge a wonderful game?

CHAPTER 14
Trumps Are Wild

Charting Your Trump Course

"When I take a fifty-fifty chance, I expect it to come off eight or nine times out of ten."

The Hideous Hog

The issue here is how to tackle these trump suits in a way that will maximize your winners.

Missing Honors	# Cards Between Declarer/Dummy	Example	Strategy
Q	8	A2 KJ6543	Take the ace, then finesse the jack.
Q and J	8	5432 AK109	Finesse the 10, hoping RHO holds the queen-jack.
Q	9	A32 KJ7654	Do not finesse. Take the ace and king.
K	10 or fewer	65432 AQJ109	Finesse. Do not play for the drop.
K	11	65432 AQJ1098	Play for the drop by leading the ace.
K and Q	8 or 9	5432 AJ109(8)	Lead low toward the jack. If it loses, finesse the 10.
K and J	9	5432 AQ1098	Finesse the queen. If it loses, play the ace.
A and J	8	5432 KQ109	Lead low toward queen. If it loses, finesse the 10.
A and J	9	65432 KQ109	Lead low toward queen. If it loses, play the king.

Drawing Trumps: Count on Your Opponents

> *"Counting to a bridge player is similar to an actor learning his lines — it does not guarantee success, but he cannot succeed without it."*
>
> *George S. Kaufman, playwright, director and bridge player*

Counting trumps should be a straightforward process. However, most players do it the hard way. Here is the simple, yet effective technique used by experienced players.

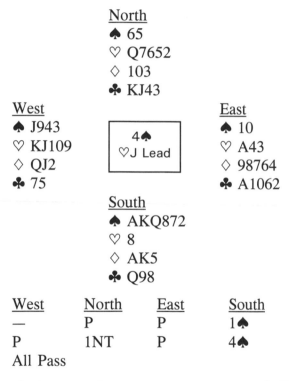

North
♠ 65
♡ Q7652
♢ 103
♣ KJ43

West
♠ J943
♡ KJ109
♢ QJ2
♣ 75

4♠
♡J Lead

East
♠ 10
♡ A43
♢ 98764
♣ A1062

South
♠ AKQ872
♡ 8
♢ AK5
♣ Q98

West	North	East	South
—	P	P	1♠
P	1NT	P	4♠
All Pass			

With only two sure losers, prospects are good. The ♡J is led, and it is time to think about the opponents' trumps. You have six spades and dummy has two, a total of eight. Therefore, the opponents have five.

After winning the ♡J, West leads a second heart which you ruff. **You do not need to keep track of that trump**. The opponents began the hand with five, and they still have all of those. Don't draw trumps just yet. First things first.

You must ruff your ◇5 while dummy retains some trumps. You cash the ◇AK and ruff a diamond with the ♠5. **You need not worry about that trump either**. The opponents' five spades are still intact.

Now you are ready to draw trumps. Lead a spade to your ace as both opponents follow suit. Two down, three to go. When you continue with the king, East discards a diamond. You know that West has two trumps remaining, since only three of the opponents' five spades have been accounted for.

Take the ♠Q, pulling one more trump from West. You now leave him with his trump winner, and establish clubs. Your only losers are one heart, one spade, and the ♣A.

Voids Are the Name of the Game

For a little fun, consider the following: What is the fewest number of HCP needed by one side to make a grand slam? (Hint: You have only two opposing trumps to count, and each royal member is single.)

North
♠ —
♡ 97643
◇ 432
♣ 65432

South
♠ 8765432
♡ AJ10852
◇ —
♣ —

The answer is five. 7♡ is cold as long as trumps are divided 1–1 and neither opponent has five spades. You will ruff spades until you have established them.

Dummy's Ruff Can Be Smooth

"Shortness is in the eye of the beholder."

Wee Willie Keeler, 19th century baseball player

Many players do not appreciate the importance of winning extra tricks with *dummy's* trumps. Of course, this is possible only when dummy has a short suit along with adequate trumps.

On this deal, declarer was not impressed with any of dummy's suits.

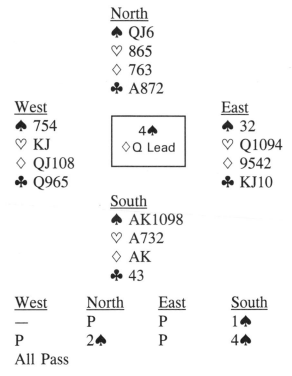

North
♠ QJ6
♡ 865
◇ 763
♣ A872

West
♠ 754
♡ KJ
◇ QJ108
♣ Q965

4♠
◇Q Lead

East
♠ 32
♡ Q1094
◇ 9542
♣ KJ10

South
♠ AK1098
♡ A732
◇ AK
♣ 43

West	North	East	South
—	P	P	1♠
P	2♠	P	4♠
All Pass			

Declarer won the diamond lead and drew trumps in three rounds. He now turned his attention to hearts, hoping for a 3-3 split. After the normal 4-2 heart split, declarer ended with the same nine winners he had at the start. However, he could have made 4♠.

While dummy is not short in hearts, he does have fewer than declarer. With that in mind, declarer should trump one of his heart losers in dummy for the tenth trick.

Use good crossruff technique by taking your side-suit winners first.

Trick 1:   Win your ◇A.
Trick 2:   Lead your ◇K.
Trick 3:   Lead a club to the ace.
Trick 4:   Lead a heart to your ace.
Trick 5:   Concede a heart trick.
Trick 6:   Win the likely trump return in your hand. No other defense
            would affect the outcome.
Trick 7:   Concede a second heart, creating a void in dummy (*finally*).
Trick 8:   Win the trump return in your hand.
Trick 9:   Ruff your losing heart with dummy's ♠Q. *Más vale tarde que
            nunca.* That translates to *better late than never*, which is all I
            remember from three years of high school Spanish.

At this point, you have won seven tricks. You still have three high
trumps in your hand. In addition to your four obvious side-suit winners,
your ruff in dummy increased your five trump winners to six. All you lose
is one club and two hearts. Very smooth!

Drawing Trumps First is Often the Worst

Just as a golf or tennis pro must work on correcting a student's swing, a bridge teacher must often correct a student's misconceptions. Whatever the source, many players carry around a great deal of incomplete and/or incorrect information. You have heard it all before:

"An opening 1♣ bid is usually made with a three-card suit."

"The Rule of 11 only works in notrump."

"You need an opening hand to answer partner's preempt."

I have always been struck by the irony of the following scenario. Someone calls, seeking bridge lessons. We agree on all the administrative details. He then announces, "There's just one problem. I've never played bridge before. I am a total beginner."

My reaction: "Problem? What problem? You're fortunate to be starting fresh — no bad habits to undo. What could be better?"

Perhaps the most popular bridge misconception is that declarer should draw trumps first. Wrong! I do not know why so many players believe this when the truth is: **With most hands, it is wrong to begin, let alone finish drawing the opponents' trumps as soon as possible.**

It would be absurd to say that drawing trumps first is never correct. However, there are many reasons to postpone pulling trump, such as:

1. You need to ruff losers in dummy.

2. You must preserve trump entries in order to develop a long suit or set up an endplay.

3. You are eager to set up a side suit on which you will discard losers.

In fact I would estimate that declarer should draw trumps first roughly 40 percent of the time.

As South, can you take 10 tricks on the following deal?

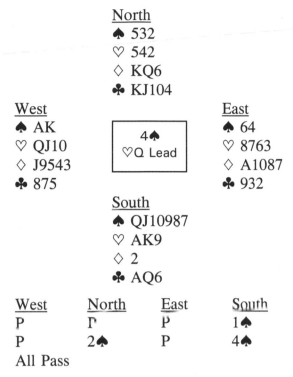

North
- ♠ 532
- ♡ 542
- ◇ KQ6
- ♣ KJ104

West
- ♠ AK
- ♡ QJ10
- ◇ J9543
- ♣ 875

4♠
♡Q Lead

East
- ♠ 64
- ♡ 8763
- ◇ A1087
- ♣ 932

South
- ♠ QJ10987
- ♡ AK9
- ◇ 2
- ♣ AQ6

West	North	East	South
P	Γ	P	1♠
P	2♠	P	4♠
All Pass			

Declarer is confronted with four possible losers: two spade tricks, one heart and one diamond. Clearly, there is nothing he can do about the ace and king of trumps. The diamond loser is also inevitable, unless the opponents neglect to take their ace. Therefore, declarer should focus his attention on avoiding the heart loser.

Some players are overly impressed with the quality of the club suit. They immediately attack trumps, planning to discard the heart loser on dummy's fourth club. This cannot possibly succeed.

Give it a try. You (South) win the heart and play a trump. West takes the ♠K and leads a second heart. You win and play a second trump, giving West the lead. He cashes the ♡10 and shifts to a diamond. Down one. No, after the heart lead, dummy's fourth club is not the answer.

(Deal repeated for convenience)

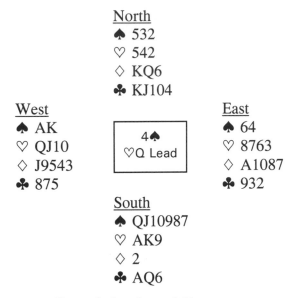

North
♠ 532
♡ 542
◇ KQ6
♣ KJ104

West
♠ AK
♡ QJ10
◇ J9543
♣ 875

4♠
♡Q Lead

East
♠ 64
♡ 8763
◇ A1087
♣ 932

South
♠ QJ10987
♡ AK9
◇ 2
♣ AQ6

The correct line of play is as follows:

Trick 1:   Win the ♡Q lead with the ace.
Trick 2:   Lead a diamond to the king and ace. You need to develop a
           diamond winner; until you force out the ace, dummy's
           diamonds are worthless.
Trick 3:   Win East's heart return with your king.
Trick 4:   Play the ♣6 to dummy's king.
Trick 5:   Cash dummy's ◇Q, discarding the ♡9 from your hand.
Trick 6:   Draw trumps, conceding the ace and king.

It never ceases to amaze me what is possible when you don't draw
trumps first. I know that it is difficult to undo the habits of a lifetime, but
why not start today?

Maneuvering Trump Entries Like a Virtuoso

Drawing trumps with a long, solid suit is not difficult, but neither should it be considered routine. By exercising a bit of care and effort, you can maintain great flexibility while pulling trumps:

North
QJ53

South
AK10862

Assume that, as expected, trumps divide 2-1. If you play the AK while following low from dummy, you will find yourself with:

North
QJ

South
10862

Very inflexible; there are no entries to the South hand. If, instead, you cash the QJ while following low from your hand, the result will be:

North
53

South
AK108

Equally inflexible; now you cannot enter the North hand.

Start again. Take the ace and lead the six to the queen (among other equivalent solutions). You have preserved:

North
J5

South
K1082

You now have two entries to each hand.

You lose nothing with this approach, and you will be a hero if you need the entries later.

On the following deal, declarer did not appreciate dummy's two entries, and paid the price.

North
♠ 8754
♡ 1086
♢ 965
♣ 754

West
♠ 103
♡ 3
♢ KQJ83
♣ J9632

4♡
♢K Lead

East
♠ K962
♡ A54
♢ A742
♣ Q10

South
♠ AQJ
♡ KQJ972
♢ 10
♣ AK8

West	North	East	South
—	—	1♢	Dbl
3♢*	P	P	4♡
All Pass			

Weak jump raise.

West led the ♢K and continued with the queen. Declarer ruffed with the ♡2, but he could no longer make the hand. When he continued with the ♡K, East knew enough to hold up; what was his hurry? It was now impossible for declarer to enter dummy more than once, and one successful spade finesse was not enough. Declarer eventually lost a spade trick for down one.

Declarer was unlucky to be playing against a capable defender, but good players make their own luck. If South had ruffed with an honor instead of the deuce at trick two, he could have forced two entries to dummy, as follows. Lead the ♡2 to dummy's six. If East wins his ace, the trump position will be:

North
♡ 108

West   East
♡ —   ♡ 54

South
♡ KQ97

Once declarer is careful to trump East's diamond return with a second honor, he is in control. Trumping with honors is not showing off; sometimes it is the only way to preserve entries. After South ruffs high, he leads the ♡7 to the 8 and takes the spade finesse. When that wins, he repeats the maneuver; ♡9 to the 10 for a second spade finesse.

It would not have helped East to duck dummy's ♡6 on the first round of trumps. Now the lead would be in dummy, allowing an immediate spade finesse. The position would then be:

North
♡ 108

West   East
♡ —   ♡ A5

South
♡ KQ97

This layout is virtually the same as above, except for East's ace. Again, no problem: ♡7 to the 8 and East's ace; trump the diamond high; and lead the ♡9 to dummy's 10 for the second spade finesse.

It is Not Illegal to Count Winners in a Suit Contract

You've heard it a thousand times: "In notrump, count winners; in suit contracts, count losers." Or, as I like to remind my students, use the consonants in *"win"* and *"lose"* as a memory aid — *W*inners in *N*otrump, *L*osers in *S*uit contracts.

However, sometimes it is easier and more helpful to count winners in a suit contract. This is especially true when the contract is a partscore or slam; the trump suit is shaky; or the hand involves a crossruff. On this hand, South demonstrated that he could count to ten:

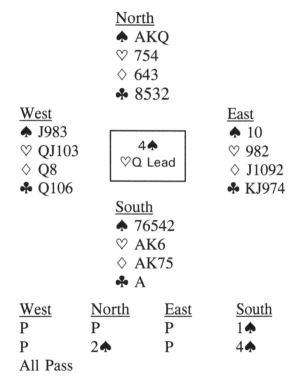

North
♠ AKQ
♡ 754
◇ 643
♣ 8532

West
♠ J983
♡ QJ103
◇ Q8
♣ Q106

4♠
♡Q Lead

East
♠ 10
♡ 982
◇ J1092
♣ KJ974

South
♠ 76542
♡ AK6
◇ AK75
♣ A

West	North	East	South
P	P	P	1♠
P	2♠	P	4♠
All Pass			

Declarer counted eight winners: ♡AK, ◇AK, ♣A and ♠AKQ. If spades divided 3–2, declarer's last two trumps would be good. However, good players prefer good technique to good splits and good fortune.

After winning the heart lead, South took his ♣A. Next, he cashed the ♠AK. Bad split. No problem! He ruffed a club, and led a third trump. A second club ruff provided declarer's seventh trick. ◇AK, ♡K and on to the next hand.

CHAPTER 15
Declarer's Tricks and Traps

Help Your Opponents Take the Bait

"If you do not force your opponents to make mistakes, you cannot win."

Marty Bergen

Face facts. Most bridge players are honor-coverers. When declarer leads an honor through your average defender, he will invariably cover it whenever he has a higher honor. This is usually not best. A defender's mindset should be:

> **Cover an honor with an honor only when you have a realistic chance of promoting a card in your hand or partner's.**

Even if your opponent knows not to cover, he will usually hesitate to mull it over. Declarer is certainly entitled to draw inferences from the opponents' actions. In bridge, unlike poker, a player is not permitted to bluff by deliberately hesitating.

For the most part, only very good players can duck smoothly when an honor is led through them. Against these players, you cannot make assumptions. With everyone else, it is reasonable to infer that:

1. If your opponent has a higher card, he will either cover or hesitate before playing.

2. If your opponent calmly plays low, he does not have a higher honor.

Are you intrigued by this game within the game? Food for thought. For now, I would like to concentrate on inducing covers in long suits. Suppose this is your trump suit:

North (dummy)
Q764

South
AJ10853

The best chance to avoid a loser with 10 cards missing the king, is to finesse. Many players believe that it is correct to play the ace, hoping to drop the singleton king, but that is not the percentage play.

You can improve your chances by entering dummy and leading the queen. Most Easts will cover with the king whenever they hold it, or pause to think, marking them with that card. If an average player sitting East smoothly plays low, assume that he does not have the king. Your only chance is to rise with the ace, hoping to drop West's king. Of course, when an expert calmly plays low, you cannot take any inference; go with the odds and finesse.

North
Q8653

South
AJ10974

With an eleventh trump, it is correct to play for the drop. Once again, make sure to lead the queen from dummy. Give the people what they want — if East likes to cover, it would be a shame to deny him the chance to do his thing. How about:

North
A743

South
KJ109

This is an annoying two-way guess finesse. With eight cards missing the queen, you should intend to finesse. ("Eight ever, nine never" is okay in general.) However, you can finesse either way, depending on who you think has the queen. Sometimes the bidding will provide clues, other times you are on your own.

Try leading the jack. If West covers, your problems are over. If he stops to think, assume he has the lady. If he ducks smoothly, it is reasonable to assume that East has the queen. Rise with the ace and finesse through East. Against average opponents, you will guess correctly much more than 50% of the time.

Here is another layout where you have the opportunity to take advantage of your opponents' covering tendencies.

North
10543

South
A9862

This appears to be a boring suit. If the four missing cards divide 2–2, you will lose only one trick. However, if they divide 3–1, which is more likely, you will lose two. Now, watch the magic of "where there's a coverer, there's a way." After entering dummy in another suit, lead the 10. If East has QJ7, KJ7, or KQ7 and makes the mistake of covering, your ace will capture two honors when West follows with his singleton honor. Not only will you restrict your losses to one trick, but you will enjoy a psychological advantage on the next hand.

Do I have any regrets about profiting from my opponents' errors? Nope, not at all. When I played competitive tennis, I dreamed about concluding a match with a spectacular winner. In reality, many of my victories ended with an opponent's double fault. I do not know how you would feel, but I slept just fine.

"It's not enough to win the tricks that belong to you. Try also for some that belong to the opponents."

Alfred Sheinwold

Some Expensive Advice

"Bridge mirrors every facet of life."

Victor Mollo, British writer

I am frequently asked about bridge hands and am more than willing to answer. It is gratifying to help others understand the nuances of this wonderful game. On the other hand, it is annoying when the player:

1. Interrupts a conversation in progress.

2. Is not interested in learning but simply wants to hear that an expert has agreed with him.

3. Asks what I would bid with partner's hand; then, if I happen to agree with his absent partner, attempts to convince me why I am wrong.

Along those lines: A player approaches a bridge professional to ask a question. The pro answers, and the player thanks him and moves along.

Three days later, the player receives a bill in the mail for $100 from the pro. He is outraged and immediately calls up his attorney. "What nerve! Can you believe him? All I did was ask one question!"

His attorney responds, "I understand, but look at the situation from his point of view. The man was at work, and you asked him to render his professional services. I'm afraid you must pay the fee."

"Oh all right. I don't agree with you, but I see where you are coming from. That will be the last time I ask a bridge pro for his opinion. Thank you for your advice."

Quite reluctantly, he sends a check to the bridge professional. Three days later our hero receives a bill for $150 from his lawyer!

Life is Pleasing When You Start Squeezing

"A well-played bridge hand has as much power to thrill and to satisfy as a Beethoven symphony."

Hugh Kelsey, prolific Scottish bridge writer

For many players, the most fascinating and exciting of the so-called advanced plays is the squeeze. It has acquired an unwarranted mystique and is perceived as being too difficult for the average player. There are some very complex squeezes, but the truth is that **the basic squeeze can be executed by anyone**. The best way to approach this topic is with questions and answers. Let's do it:

1. *When should a squeeze be attempted?*

   When there is no other way to get rid of a loser. The outlook is bleak, so there is nothing to lose by hoping for a squeeze.

   The opportunity for a squeeze knows no limits. Notrump and suit contracts are both fair game. In addition, squeezes can be applied whether the extra trick fulfills the contract or produces an overtrick.

2. *What must declarer do?*

   A. Take all his winners in the irrelevant suits and hope for a miracle. The irrelevant suits are those in which declarer has no chance of creating an extra winner. An example of an irrelevant suit is one in which the opponents are void, such as trumps.

   B. Suppose you have a suit such as A9 opposite dummy's K5. If either hand held a third card, perhaps A9 opposite K75, there would be some hope of winning a third trick in this suit — now it would become *relevant*. The third card is called a threat card (or menace) because its mere presence threatens the opponents. One of them must hold onto at least three cards in that suit to prevent your seven from becoming a winner.

3. *I have a menace — so what?*

A. Keep the lines of communication open between declarer's hand and dummy. It does not help you if the opponent's discard establishes a winner that you cannot reach.

B. Keep an eye on the opponents' discards. Fortunately, with most basic squeezes, you only need to keep track of what is being discarded in the relevant suit(s).

4. *What are you hoping for?*

A discarding mistake would not bother you at all. Discarding is often difficult, tedious and annoying. The more discards you squeeze out of your opponents, the greater the chance they will make an error. The result of this discarding error is a *pseudo squeeze*.

When you cash your last winner in the irrelevant suit(s), you hope that an opponent will be forced to discard a winner from a relevant suit. These are *legitimate squeezes*.

5. *How often do squeezes occur?*

More often than you think. I cannot tell you how often I have been aware of an upcoming squeeze while watching as dummy — if only declarer would cash his last winner. In addition, the potential for a pseudo squeeze is present on every deal.

It is even possible for the defending side to execute a squeeze. There are also occasions when one defender squeezes his partner. By the way, squeezing your partner is definitely frowned upon.

6. *Why are squeezes so difficult?*

They do not have to be. Remember:

✓ Discarding is very difficult for everyone. Get into the habit of making the opponents sweat.

✓ Bridge is not like pinochle; you don't receive a bonus for winning the last trick.

✓ Never give up. No matter how obvious your loser is, any chance is better than none.

Observe how the noose tightens around West:

North
♠ 5432
♡ Q985
◇ A5
♣ AK2

West
♠ AK107
♡ 10
◇ 932
♣ 109873

```
┌─────────┐
│   4♡    │
│ ♠A Lead │
└─────────┘
```

East
♠ 98
♡ 432
◇ QJ10864
♣ QJ

South
♠ QJ6
♡ AKJ76
◇ K7
♣ 654

West	North	East	South
—	—	—	1♡
P	3NT*	P	4♡
All Pass			

* A forcing heart raise.

West led the ♠A and naturally continued with the king, followed by a third spade for partner to ruff. Declarer knew that West still had a higher spade than dummy. South needed the rest of the tricks, but was looking at an inevitable club loser. However, he did believe in squeezes, and knew enough not to give up.

Declarer won East's ◇Q return with his king, and drew two rounds of trumps. South cashed his ◇A, the irrelevant suit, and continued trumps. He knew not to touch clubs, a relevant suit. Declarer made sure to win the fourth trump in his hand in order to lead his last trump. He had no idea whether a squeeze would operate and did not need to watch or count all the discards. He only needed to observe whether West might slip and discard his winning spade.

Here was the position as declarer led his last trump:

North
♠ 5
♡ —
♢ —
♣ AK2

West
♠ 10
♡ —
♢ —
♣ 1098

East (immaterial)
♠ —
♡ —
♢ J10
♣ QJ

South
♠ —
♡ 7
♢ —
♣ 654

West was squeezed on the play of the ♡7 because East couldn't guard clubs. When West threw a club, declarer discarded dummy's ♠5; there was no point in keeping it once West kept his spade. Declarer now led clubs and hoped for the best. Because of the fortunate club distribution, his prayers were answered. Of course, if West had discarded his spade, declarer would have kept dummy's winning five.

West could have done nothing in the endgame. The best players in the world are at your mercy when the cards cooperate.

Squeezes will always be a very satisfying part of the game. One of my favorite teaching moments occurred many years ago when my phone rang at about 12:30 a.m. To my surprise, it was one of my students. "I hope that I'm not waking you, Marty, but I just *had* to call."

"No problem, Kitty. Are you okay?"

"Oh yes, wonderful. I was playing bridge, and I just executed my first squeeze. I haven't been so excited since the birth of my first child!"

Is Bridge a Mathematical Game?

"Fascinating in so many other ways, there is one aspect of bridge that bores me intensely — the pursuit of hair-splitting percentages and abstract probabilities."

Victor Mollo

Many players believe that bridge is a mathematical game — not true. While arithmetic is involved in many bridge decisions, the numbers are rarely larger than 26. What bridge *is* all about is logic and reasoning.

If a player passes his partner's opening bid of one in a suit, he should have fewer than six points. If that player shows up with an ace during the play, you will expect any missing queens to be held by his partner. Higher math rarely enters the picture.

There is one elementary mathematical principle, however, that you must know — basic percentages. When you lead low toward the AQ, the king will be located favorably half the time. A simple finesse, then, has a 50% chance of success.

Basic percentages play a significant role in understanding the likely distribution of the opponents' cards. Do not fret — this will prove to be an easy topic to learn. Here are the important principles:

1. **When you are missing an odd number of cards, expect them to divide as evenly as possible**. If you are declarer with a combined eight-card fit, the opponents have five cards. You cannot expect them to divide 2½–2½; therefore expect 3–2. The same holds true when your side has 10 cards. Their three are probably divided 2–1.

2. However, **when you are missing an even number of cards, do not expect them to divide perfectly**. If your side has a total of seven cards, their six will only divide evenly (3–3) 35.53% of the time. It is unlikely that one player will hold five cards. You should expect the suit to split 4–2.

You are now armed with all the mathematics you will ever need. How can you apply your new-found knowledge? Declare the following hand, and show your stuff.

North
♠ AKQJ9
♡ 432
◇ 65
♣ 843

┌─────────────┐
│   4♠   │
│ ♡K Lead   │
└─────────────┘

South
♠ 6542
♡ J106
◇ AQ
♣ AKQ6

West	North	East	South
—	P	P	1NT
P	2♡*	P	2♠
P	3NT	P	4♠
All Pass			

* *Jacoby transfer*, showing five or more spades.

West led the ♡K, and East encouraged with the nine. West played another heart to East's ace. East now continued the annoyingly accurate defense by shifting to the ◇10.

South was at the crossroads. To finesse or not to finesse, that is the question. What would you do?

The opponents have an even number of clubs — you do not expect them to divide evenly. Therefore, your fourth club is probably worthless. Accordingly, finesse the ◇Q.

Try this layout:

North
♠ AKQJ9
♡ 432
◇ 65
♣ 843

┌─────────────┐
│   4♠   │
│ ♡K Lead   │
└─────────────┘

South
♠ 654
♡ J106
◇ AQ
♣ AKQ62

West	North	East	South
—	P	P	1NT
P	2♡*	P	2♠
P	3NT	P	4♠
All Pass			

* *Jacoby transfer*, showing five or more spades.

West leads the ♡K, East contributes the 9. West plays a heart to East's ace and East shifts to the ◇10.

You have eight clubs (wasn't there a song, "What a difference a *club* makes?"), and the opponents have only five. **Do not finesse; their clubs are probably divided 3–2 (67.83%).** You expect to be able to run clubs and discard dummy's red-suit losers. In addition, if clubs had been divided 4–1, the player with the singleton would probably have led it.

Win the ◇A and play five rounds of trumps. With your clubs concealed, you have the extra chance that an opponent might err and discard one on the run of dummy's trumps.

Obviously, these two deals are a matched pair. In both, you would have preferred to have the time to test clubs first. After East's tough defense, you were forced to commit yourself in diamonds before discovering how the clubs split.

Bridge mathematics is an overrated concern. Just remember:

> **An odd number of cards usually divides evenly. An even number usually does not.**

Please keep in mind that these are not guarantees, only probabilities.

I was recently told the following story by a tournament director. One of my students called him to the table in a snit.

"What's the problem," the director asked.

"There is something wrong with these cards," the player complained. The director checked the cards, and as expected, they were okay.

"What is the problem?" asked the director patiently.

"I was playing 3NT, and the key suit divided 3–3. I didn't play for that and I got a bad result. My teacher told me that *six cards never divide perfectly*. It's not fair."

Oh well. My father always wanted me to be a lawyer.

CHAPTER 16
Defense: Do a Lot With a Little

Force Declarer to Trump — Absolutely!

The opponents bid to a contract of 4♠. You lead the ◇A, partner encourages with the 10 as declarer drops the jack. Here is the layout of the diamonds in view:

North
◇ 7543

You   Partner
◇ AK82   ◇ 10

South
◇ J

You happily continue with the king, which declarer trumps with the ♠2. Which of the following best expresses your feelings at the moment?

1. You wish you had led something else.

2. You are angry with partner for encouraging without shortness.

3. You erred in allowing declarer to win a trick with his deuce of trumps. You would take it back if you could.

4. You are pleased to have shortened declarer's trumps.

Most players respond with a combination of the first three answers. Why is that? They channel their hopes and energy into winning tricks immediately! If they cannot, *out of sight, out of mind*. Do not allow yourself to think this way.

Defensive play should be considered from a long-range perspective. Declarer's losers won't magically disappear. Good defenders proceed with a plan and wait to reap the fruits of their labor.

A key principle that should govern your defense against suit contracts:

> **Be eager to shorten the opponent's hand that is longest in trump.**

Assuming that declarer usually has trump length, it is important to understand that his trumps will always be good tricks. Declarer should not be happy when forced to part with a precious trump when he has a trump holding such as:

North
♠ 754

South
♠ KQJ102

Declarer was always going to win four spade tricks while losing one. However, if South can be forced to ruff twice, he will only be able to draw three rounds of trumps. If a defender started with four trumps, his last one will become a winner.

The defenders should continue to shorten declarer's trump, hoping that he will eventually lose control of the hand. This defensive strategy is referred to as *the forcing game*. It is especially applicable when one defender holds four trumps or has reason to believe that his partner might.

On the other hand, declarer is normally delighted to ruff in the short hand. The tricks dummy can win by ruffing represent bonus trump tricks.

Declarer must be careful to keep enough trumps in his hand to retain control. This is crucial, except when *all* trump tricks are taken separately via a crossruff. **Declarer should be eager to ruff in the short hand but reluctant to ruff with trump length**. It should come as no surprise that declarer's objectives are the opposite of the defenders'.

Take a look at the entire deal:

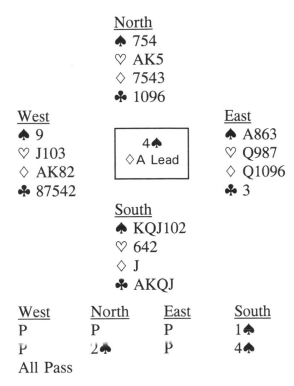

North
♠ 754
♡ AK5
◇ 7543
♣ 1096

West
♠ 9
♡ J103
◇ AK82
♣ 87542

4♠
◇A Lead

East
♠ A863
♡ Q987
◇ Q1096
♣ 3

South
♠ KQJ102
♡ 642
◇ J
♣ AKQJ

West	North	East	South
P	P	P	1♠
P	2♣	P	4♠
All Pass			

Without the diamond continuation at trick two, South would have had no problem. He could easily have drawn trumps, losing one diamond, one heart and one spade trick.

Once West forced declarer to trump, South was in trouble. He led the ♠K, losing to East's ace. East returned the ◇Q at trick four, and declarer was forced to ruff again. At this point, South had ruffed twice and drawn one round of trumps. He had two trumps remaining while East held three. In addition to declarer's original three losers, South could not shut out East's fourth spade.

The Forcing Game — look for it wherever bridge is played. I am confident you will enjoy your role. Meanwhile, the unfortunate declarer will be reduced to playing the lead in *The Crying Game*.

Hustler's Delight

"If winning is not important, then tell me why keep score?"

Klingon crew member in Star Trek, the Next Generation

I would like to show you the ultimate example of *the forcing game.* Imagine that you are dealt the following:

♠ AKQ
♡ AKQJ109
◇ —
♣ AKQJ

This is unquestionably the best hand that you will ever hold. You choose to open 7♡, which must be laydown.

You are surprised and delighted when you are doubled; how naive of your opponent to believe that he will defeat you with his ◇A. You lose no time redoubling, wondering if anyone is capable of figuring out your score (vulnerable, it would be 2940 using duplicate scoring).

As expected, your opponent leads his ◇A. Partner apologizes for being broke, but you assure him that you have matters under control.

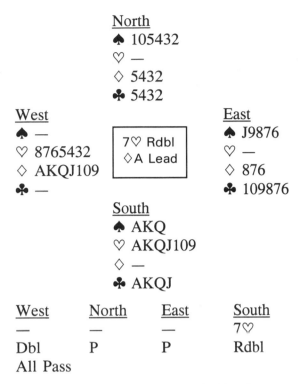

North
♠ 105432
♡ —
♢ 5432
♣ 5432

West
♠ —
♡ 8765432
♢ AKQJ109
♣ —

7♡ Rdbl
♢A Lead

East
♠ J9876
♡ —
♢ 876
♣ 109876

South
♠ AKQ
♡ AKQJ109
♢ —
♣ AKQJ

West	North	East	South
—	—	—	7♡
Dbl	P	P	Rdbl
All Pass			

Believe it or not, South can take only his six trump tricks. Every time West ruffs, he plays another diamond, forcing declarer to trump. Having lost control, South is down seven, a score of minus 4000. In fact, with repeated diamond leads, North-South cannot make any game contract!

This infamous hand is obviously rigged. South is the pigeon to be plucked, preferably in a high-stakes rubber bridge game. It is known as the Mississippi Heart Hand, because it was widely used by 19th century cardsharps[1] on Mississippi River steamboats.

Rigged or not, this deal illustrates three important bridge concepts:

1. *Points, schmoints!*

2. *The forcing game.*

3. *Length is more important than strength.* After observing the fate of West's seven small hearts versus South's six high ones, case closed.

---

[1] From *The Official Encyclopedia of Bridge, Fifth Edition* (1994). Charles M. Schwab is reported to have paid off at least $10,000 on this hand.

An Artist With a Small Canvas

"The ultimate in bridge is learning to play with poor cards."

Chip Martel, many-time world champion

A bridge hand containing no card higher than a nine is called a Yarborough, named after an English lord who would wager 1,000 pounds to one against the chance of being dealt such a hand. Lord Yarborough certainly knew what he was doing. The actual odds of such a hand are 1,827 to 1. Nowadays, *Yarborough* has been modified to describe a very bad hand, not necessarily adhering to the original requirements. Modern players would refer to the following hand as a Yarborough:

♠ 865   ♡ 643   ◇ 972   ♣ 10873

As I watched one of my best students with one of her worst hands, I could almost hear her thoughts.

"What a lousy hand," thought Jane as she gazed at:

♠ 86543
♡ 76
◇ 2
♣ 97642

"I hope that partner opens 1♠; I can't wait to jump to 4♠ and try out The Law of Total Tricks. Oh, too bad. Partner opened 1◇. So much for that. Sounds like a good time for a little R and R."

"Oh, the bidding is over already. Is it my lead? I would love to lead my singleton. Nope, I'm not on lead. Oh well, back to sleep."

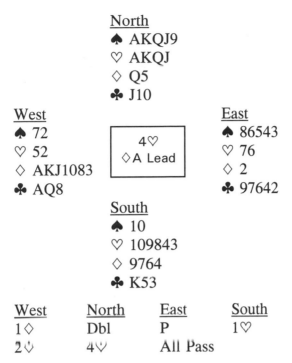

North
♠ AKQJ9
♡ AKQJ
◇ Q5
♣ J10

West
♠ 72
♡ 52
◇ AKJ1083
♣ AQ8

4♡
◇A Lead

East
♠ 86543
♡ 76
◇ 2
♣ 97642

South
♠ 10
♡ 109843
◇ 9764
♣ K53

West	North	East	South
1◇	Dbl	P	1♡
2♡	4♡	All Pass	

"Partner led the ◇A. Wow, what a dummy! 23 HCP. I'll bet South doesn't have much more than I do. Now partner is playing the ◇K; time for a discard. Let's see. I should give partner some information. I certainly don't need to tell her about my lousy spades, she can figure that suit out for herself.

"I suppose that I should let her know that I don't like clubs. I'll discard the two...

"*No, wait a minute! Wake up Janie!* It can't be right to leave partner on lead, what good would that do? Is there any hope? Maybe partner has the ♣AQ. In that case, I must lead a club *now*. Okay, ♡6, do your stuff."

There were surprised looks all around when Jane trumped her partner's ◇K. However, when she returned the ♣4, South, now frowning, was down one. With any other defense, declarer would have drawn trumps, and discarded her clubs on dummy's spades.

"You trumped my trick, partner," said West. "*Thank you!*"

Do You Believe in Magic?

Bridge can be a very aesthetic game. As in any other competitive endeavor, you must remember not to throw in the towel when the outlook is hopeless. This strategy is easy to understand but difficult to apply. With a little practice, forging ahead and making something out of nothing can become a vital part of your approach.

Whenever declarer appears to have no losers remaining in the *side suits* (suits other than trump), the defenders should try to create extra trump tricks. Consider the following:

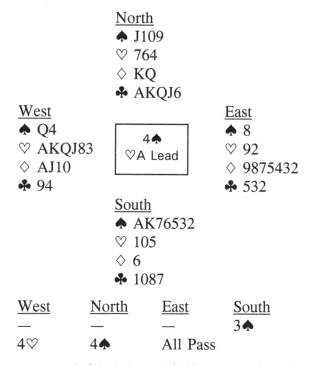

North
♠ J109
♡ 764
◇ KQ
♣ AKQJ6

West
♠ Q4
♡ AKQJ83
◇ AJ10
♣ 94

4♠
♡A Lead

East
♠ 8
♡ 92
◇ 9875432
♣ 532

South
♠ AK76532
♡ 105
◇ 6
♣ 1087

West	North	East	South
—	—	—	3♠
4♡	4♠	All Pass	

West was not thrilled about bidding game by himself, but what else could he do? However, North (a Law-abiding citizen) was always bidding 4♠ with his three-card trump support, not to mention his lovely hand.

West was not hopeful after seeing the strong dummy. When he cashed his ♡K at trick two, the heart distribution became clear. Dummy's club holding looked formidable, so West grabbed the ◇A. Now what?

With no other tricks in sight, West shifted his focus to the trump suit. He knew that declarer had seven spades for his preempt and saw five between his hand and dummy's. Therefore, East was marked with exactly one spade. West also realized that South needed the ace and king for his vulnerable preempt. However, if East had been dealt the ♠8, the defense could have presented a revival of *Eight is Enough*.

West carefully led the ♡3, making it obvious for East to trump. East's lovely eight forced declarer to overruff with the king, and West's Q4 was now good for the setting trick.

When you create a trump trick out of thin air you have delivered an *uppercut*. Do not concern yourself with remembering the word. Everyone is more impressed with a player who can execute this classy play than one who can identify it by name.

For a second opportunity to play Houdini, please turn the page.

North
♠ 965
♡ KQ64
◇ AKJ107
♣ 3

West
♠ AKQJ8
♡ 972
◇ Q4
♣ J104

```
┌─────────┐
│   4♡    │
│ ♠A Lead │
└─────────┘
```

East
♠ 43
♡ J10
◇ 9653
♣ 97652

South
♠ 1072
♡ A853
◇ 82
♣ AKQ8

West	North	East	South
—	—	P	1♣
1♠	2◇	P	2♡
P	4♡	All Pass	

West began by cashing three rounds of spades; East discarding the ♣2. West paused for thought. It was obvious that the defense would never win a trick in either minor suit. A trump trick seemed the only possibility, despite West's modest holding in the suit.

West played a fourth spade and East trumped with the 10, forcing declarer to overruff with his ace. This left the following trump position:

North
♡ KQ64

West
♡ 972

East
♡ J

South
♡ 853

Down one. The defense had created a trump trick out of thin air.

These hands do occur in real life. You may not believe in magic, but you must believe in uppercuts.

CHAPTER 17
The Defense Never Rests

When to Say No to Second Hand Low

*"...the world is full of competent declarers, but the truly expert
defender is a rare bird indeed."*

Hugh Kelsey

One basic principle of card play is *second hand low*. When you play
second to a trick, there is usually no rush to play a high card. Why?
Because your partner still has the opportunity to compete for the trick.

Second hand low, although sound advice, is only a guideline.
Sometimes logic dictates that you play second hand high. How many
exceptions are there to *second hand low*? The list is longer than you
might think. You should play second hand high in order to:

1. Take the setting trick.

2. Obtain the lead (e.g., in order to give partner a ruff).

3. Keep an opponent from winning a trick cheaply. For example, you
    have KQJx and declarer leads toward dummy's A10.

4. Win a trick that might disappear if you do not take it now.

5. Prevent declarer or dummy from winning a singleton honor.

6. Cover an honor, hoping to promote a card for your side.

7. Preserve an entry to partner's hand (usually against notrump).

Try to find the exception below:

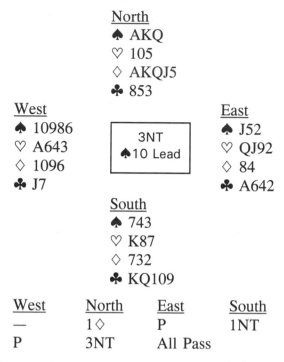

North
♠ AKQ
♡ 105
◇ AKQJ5
♣ 853

West
♠ 10986
♡ A643
◇ 1096
♣ J7

3NT
♠10 Lead

East
♠ J52
♡ QJ92
◇ 84
♣ A642

South
♠ 743
♡ K87
◇ 732
♣ KQ109

West	North	East	South
—	1◇	P	1NT
P	3NT	All Pass	

South won the opening spade lead in dummy and led a club at trick two. It would have been easy for East to play low without thought, but this East was made of sterner stuff. With eight tricks staring at him in dummy, this was no time to be blindly following maxims. If declarer held the ♡A, he had nine tricks. However, if partner held the ♡A, East could visualize the setting trick. South's 1NT response had denied a four-card major; therefore, West was known to have begun with four hearts.

East rose with his ♣A at trick two, which prevented declarer from stealing a ninth trick. He shifted to the ♡Q, which held as West signaled with the six. East continued with the ♡J, neutralizing dummy's 10.

South's goose was now crisply cooked. He covered East's ♡J but West won with the ace. West led a heart to East's nine, and the fourth round of hearts completed a superb defense.

"Nice defense, partner," said West.

"Good lead." responded East. "We had no chance if you had led your fourth-best heart. Sequences are definitely the way to go."

"Enough talk, let's play bridge," grumbled South.

Oh well, you cannot please everyone.

Second hand low is good, general advice. It is especially helpful for new players in need of guidance. However, it is important to distinguish guidelines from laws such as *you must follow suit*. Confucius say, "One who always follows low, be regarded as a schmoe."

Concentration Second to None

There is no doubt that one of the essential qualities of a good bridge player is the ability to concentrate. Bridge experts are gifted with great card sense. They also have the abilty to restrict their thoughts to bridge while playing. In fact, when experts refer to a peer as "always being *at the table*," they are extending the ultimate compliment (not commenting on the player's lack of mobility).

Of all the stories I have ever heard about great concentration, this one takes the cake. Although I would love to have been a witness, both you and I will have to be content with our imagination. Several players have verified that the following really did occur.

Terence Reese was one of England's legendary players; years ago many believed him to be the best in the world. His greatest asset was his absolute concentration. To test his intensity, a few friends set up an intriguing wager with a group of skeptics.

They hired a model to parade around Reese's table while he was declaring. In addition to being extremely attractive, she was as naked as the day she was born.

Many pounds were at stake as to Reese's reaction. Believe it or not, he never even looked up.

Now that's concentration.

You Be the Judge

"The persons who feel it necessary to conclude each hand with a magisterial correction of their partners (and their opponents as well) have no place at the bridge table, or anywhere else they might come into contact with civilized beings."

Elmer Davis, bridge writer, Harper's Magazine

A bridge partnership consists of two individuals, who invariably have different points of view. *Postmortems* are seldom dull, particularly after a disaster. Rationalization, partner-bashing and damage control are inevitable, even when the culprits are otherwise fair-minded.

A popular feature in *The Bridge World,* is "You Be The Judge" (YBTJ). A panel of experts examines deals played by other experts to determine where they went astray. As you might imagine, the analysis can become quite spirited as the panelists launch their attack. The panel also attempts to determine the most serious offense.

East-West put up an unsuccessful defense on the following hand. After observing the facts and hearing the postmortem, I would like you to play YBTJ. Picture yourself as the bridge teacher (judge) confronted by an unhappy pair of students (lawyers). I will conclude with my Supreme Court ruling (one advantage of being the author).

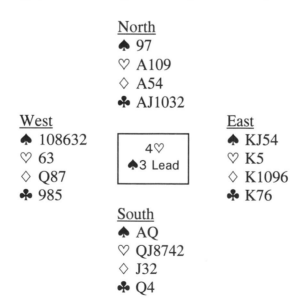

North
♠ 97
♡ A109
♢ A54
♣ AJ1032

West
♠ 108632
♡ 63
♢ Q87
♣ 985

4♡
♠3 Lead

East
♠ KJ54
♡ K5
♢ K1096
♣ K76

South
♠ AQ
♡ QJ8742
♢ J32
♣ Q4

West	North	East	South
—	1♣	P	1♡
P	2♡	P	4♡
All Pass			

Notice North's raise to 2♡ with only three hearts. A 1NT rebid is not appealing because of the worthless doubleton spade, and a 2♣ rebid would show a six-card suit.

West led the ♠3, and declarer captured East's king with his ace. South led the ♡Q at trick two, which lost to East's king. East placed the ♠Q with his partner and dutifully returned his lead. He hoped West would return a diamond to his king, and the ♣K would provide the setting trick.

South emerged with an overtrick. He won East's spade return with the queen and drew trumps. The losing club finesse was painless at this point, and declarer could discard his diamond losers on the established club suit.

Here is East-West's vigorous postmortem: "W" stands for West, "E" for East, and "S" for South.

1-E "Why did you lead your weaker suit? If you had led a diamond, they would have had no chance."

2-W "How could I know that? If you wanted a diamond lead, why didn't you bid the suit?"

3-E "I only had four diamonds. An overcall promises a five-card suit."

4-W "Not always, haven't you read *Points Schmoints*?"

5-E "Of course I have, but Marty advocates having at least three honors for an overcall in a four-card suit. In fact, his example features a suit of AKQ10. That's a far cry from K1096."

6-W "You could have shifted to a diamond after winning the ♡K. Then we would have defeated the contract despite my lead."

7-E "I know. However, if you had the ♠Q instead of the ◇Q, my defense was correct. Had I known you were a devotee of garbage leads, I might have figured that out.

"After your stupid lead, South was cold if he played clubs first. How could I find the winning defense when you misled me with your lead and declarer misplayed as well?"

8-S   "Hey, leave me out of this. I played the hand correctly. It was normal to draw trumps first on this hand."

That was quite a postmortem. If East-West had devoted as much energy to defending the hand as they did to defending themselves, they would have defeated the contract.

(Deal repeated for convenience)

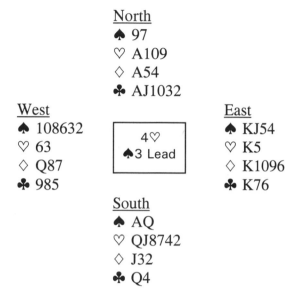

North
♠ 97
♡ A109
◇ A54
♣ AJ1032

West
♠ 108632
♡ 63
◇ Q87
♣ 985

4♡
♠3 Lead

East
♠ KJ54
♡ K5
◇ K1096
♣ K76

South
♠ AQ
♡ QJ8742
◇ J32
♣ Q4

Have you completed your YBTJ analysis? Now it's my turn.

1.   West should have preferred the more aggressive diamond lead.

2.   An opening diamond lead was certainly not obvious.

3.   An overcall usually promises at least five cards.

4.   Yes, a one-level overcall can be made on a very strong four-card suit.

5.   You should have three honors when you overcall in a four-card suit. I would not have bid 1◇. East has a very flexible hand, with honors in all suits. He has no reason to direct partner's attention toward any specific suit.

6.   Yes, a shift to the ◇10 would have defeated the contract.

7. East is correct: A spade continuation would be necessary if West's queens were reversed. Yes, South would have always made the hand if he had played clubs first. Although the club finesse would lose, declarer would discard a diamond loser on the third round of clubs.

8. South's actual line of play was normal and correct. The only reason to play clubs at trick two would be if they split 3–3 *and* both finesses were destined to fail. This definitely goes against the odds.

What gets my vote for the worst transgression? Would you believe it didn't even get mentioned? At the first trick, East should have played the ♠J instead of the king. There is no risk because declarer is marked with the ace; partner would never underlead an ace at trick one against a suit contract. If declarer had the AQ, he deserved to win two tricks.

The play of the jack from KJ against suit contracts is an example of a *discovery play*. It will enable East to discover immediately who holds the queen. (If declarer wins the ace, West obviously has the queen.)

Observe how this play simplifies matters for the defense. Once East learns that there are no spade tricks available, the menacing club suit makes it clear that a diamond shift is necessary. After East leads the ◇10, declarer cannot make the hand against correct defense.

In conclusion:

1. Reread "21 Rules Of Being a Good Partner," especially numbers 1, 3, 4, 5 and 13.

2. Use your energy for thinking during the play, rather than rationalizing in the postmortem.

3. When defending against suit contracts, remember the third-hand play of the jack from KJ.

If Declarer Smart, Defender Not

"Never reproach your partner if there is the slightest thing for which you can reproach yourself."

Ely Culbertson

If your opponents are consistently bidding to the best contract, you may not be competing and preempting enough. If declarer is playing too skillfully, perhaps you are not putting up a challenging enough defense.

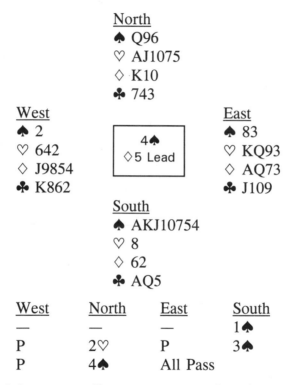

North
♠ Q96
♡ AJ1075
◇ K10
♣ 743

West
♠ 2
♡ 642
◇ J9854
♣ K862

4♠
◇5 Lead

East
♠ 83
♡ KQ93
◇ AQ73
♣ J109

South
♠ AKJ10754
♡ 8
◇ 62
♣ AQ5

West	North	East	South
—	—	—	1♠
P	2♡	P	3♠
P	4♠	All Pass	

The defense was off to a great start after dummy's ◇K was captured by the ace. East cashed the ◇Q for the second defensive trick and made the obvious shift to the ♣J, attacking dummy's weakness.

Declarer was in no hurry to finesse; he had spotted an attractive alternative. Of course, if East held the ♣K, South would still have time to establish a second club trick. After grabbing the ♣A, declarer set out to develop dummy's heart suit.

South led a heart to the ace, and ruffed a heart with the ♠J. He then led the ♠7 to the nine, and ruffed another heart with the ♠K. It was now easy to cross to dummy with a trump to ruff East's ♡K with the trump ace. A low spade to dummy's six allowed declarer to cash the winning ♡J and discard the ♣5. Declarer's only remaining loser was the ♣Q.

"Well played, partner," said North.

"Thanks for the five-card suit," responded South, "and for the three trump entries. I would have gone down if your ♠6 had been the two."

"Good lead, partner," said East. "If you had led a club, declarer would have made an overtrick."

"Thank you." said West. "It's too bad declarer didn't finesse when you returned a club. Oh well, *we* were never going to defeat this contract. It's my turn to deal."

And on to the next hand they went.

Time out. Are you ready to move on? While I hope that you would have played as skillfully as declarer, I am not ready to move on. Should South have been allowed to play this well?

After winning the first two diamond tricks, East couldn't wait to attack clubs, dummy's weak suit. What was his hurry? If declarer had club losers, his only hope would be to set up hearts.

East knew that declarer could not use dummy's heart *strength* because of his own imposing hearts. East should have guaranteed that South could never use dummy's heart *length* by returning a trump at trick three. With only two trump entries remaining in dummy, South would be unable to establish dummy's suit.

Little did West realize how accurate he was being with his "*we* were never going to defeat this contract" statement. Would he have done better with *you* as his partner?

Give Partner the Signal

Most experts, if asked, are quick to explain suit-preference signals. They emphasize that unlike all other defensive signals, **suit preference is usually given by the person leading to the trick**. Perhaps it might be more helpful if they were called *suit-preference leads*.

Suit-preference signals are ideal when you are attempting to give partner a ruff. How can he find you so you can give him another ruff? Observe the suit-preference signal in action:

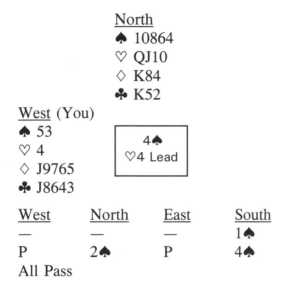

North
♠ 10864
♡ QJ10
◇ K84
♣ K52

West (You)
♠ 53
♡ 4
◇ J9765
♣ J8643

4♠
♡4 Lead

West	North	East	South
—	—	—	1♠
P	2♠	P	4♠
All Pass			

You lead the ♡4 and are delighted when your partner wins the ace. You ruff his heart return. The defense is off to a great start. Now what?

If partner has a minor-suit ace, you need only to lead that suit. He can then give you a second ruff to defeat the contract. However, if you know what suit to return from the facts given, you are amazingly gifted.

The answer to the riddle, "Where, oh where, is partner's ace?" can be found by examining the card he returned! Suppose that partner started with ♡A9732. After winning the ♡A, he has four cards available to lead back for you to trump (he hopes). The card he leads will tell you which suit he prefers.

Take a look at the entire deal:

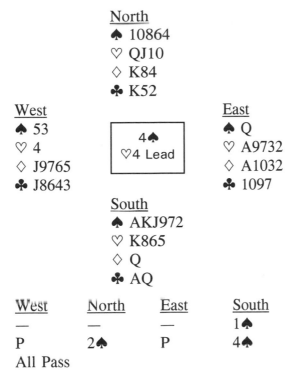

North
♠ 10864
♡ QJ10
◇ K84
♣ K52

West
♠ 53
♡ 4
◇ J9765
♣ J8643

4♠
♡4 Lead

East
♠ Q
♡ A9732
◇ A1032
♣ 1097

South
♠ AKJ972
♡ K865
◇ Q
♣ AQ

West	North	East	South
—	—	—	1♠
P	2♠	P	4♠
All Pass			

With this heart holding, East will return the nine, his highest spot card. This commands you to lead diamonds, the higher-ranking of the two side suits. If his ace had been in clubs, he would have led back the ♡2. In either case you will happily comply, delighted to receive the direction.

Any partnership will be doing well if both players understand basic suit-preference signals. They can be used in a variety of situations.

Consider the following deal:

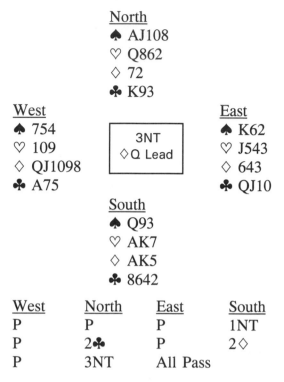

North
♠ AJ108
♡ Q862
♢ 72
♣ K93

West
♠ 754
♡ 109
♢ QJ1098
♣ A75

3NT
♢Q Lead

East
♠ K62
♡ J543
♢ 643
♣ QJ10

South
♠ Q93
♡ AK7
♢ AK5
♣ 8642

West	North	East	South
P	P	P	1NT
P	2♣	P	2♢
P	3NT	All Pass	

Declarer won the ♢Q opening lead with his king. He then led the
♠Q, losing to East's king. East fired back the ♢6, which declarer ducked.
West won this with his eight and returned the nine to declarer's ace.

Declarer cashed dummy's three spade winners, and the spotlight
turned to East as he considered his discard. Reluctant to part with a club
honor, East sluffed a heart. Declarer now cashed the ♡A, ♡K and ♡Q,
dropping East's jack. Dummy's ♡8 produced the ninth trick because of
East's error. Making 3NT.

Go back to trick three when West was left with the ♢J109. He could
have led any of those cards to knock out South's ace. Therefore, the card
West chose to lead here gave suit preference. When West led the ♢9 as
opposed to the jack or ten, East should have known that partner's entry
was in clubs, not hearts. This should have made it clear to East that his
clubs were immaterial.

The following deal reinforces the principle of suit-preference signals when you are establishing your suit against notrump contracts:

North
♠ J9
♡ Q106
♢ J104
♣ KQJ106

West
♠ Q10874
♡ A54
♢ 63
♣ 432

3NT
♠7 Lead

East
♠ K52
♡ 98732
♢ 9875
♣ A

South
♠ A63
♡ KJ
♢ AKQ2
♣ 9875

West	North	East	South
—	—	P	1NT
P	3NT	All Pass	

Trick 1:   ♠7 to jack, king and three
Trick 2:   ♠5 to 6, 10 and 9
Trick 3:   ♠Q (*high*) to drive out the ace.

When East wins his ♣A, he knows that partner likes hearts. West will win the heart return, and cash two spades to defeat the contract.

Suit-preference signals can also be used in special situations when partner is on lead. Consider the following hand, where the suit-preference card is truly a signal, not a lead. (This was adapted from Philip Alder's article in *The Bulletin*, October 1990.)

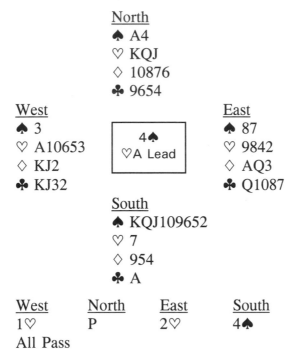

North
- ♠ A4
- ♡ KQJ
- ◇ 10876
- ♣ 9654

West
- ♠ 3
- ♡ A10653
- ◇ KJ2
- ♣ KJ32

4♠
♡A Lead

East
- ♠ 87
- ♡ 9842
- ◇ AQ3
- ♣ Q1087

South
- ♠ KQJ109652
- ♡ 7
- ◇ 954
- ♣ A

West	North	East	South
1♡	P	2♡	4♠
All Pass			

With no attractive alternative, West led the ♡A. Because dummy's hearts were now set up, a shift was in order. The defense needed to cash their tricks before South could discard his losers on the ♡KQ. West had no idea which minor partner had strength in, so East told him with a suit-preference signal. East expressed his preference for diamonds by signaling with the ♡9.

West loyally shifted to the ◇2. East won his ace and returned a diamond. The defense prevailed with three diamond tricks and the ♡A.

Suit-preference signals can be just what the doctor ordered, but they apply only in specific situations. Attitude and count signals occur more frequently. After learning suit-preference signals, many players interpret all twos as asking for clubs and nines for spades. Do not overreact this way. Most leads refer only to the player's holding in that suit.

Players who signal well are few and far between. Their dance cards will always be full and they will be more sought after than Cleopatra.

CHAPTER 18
Discarding: Throw Losers, Keep Winners

Give to Charity But Keep Parity

A difficult aspect of defense is deciding what to discard. This is especially true when one defender has several suits that need protecting. In fact, my worst bridge nightmare is a situation like this:

I'm on lead after 1NT (16–18) – P – 6NT. My hand is:

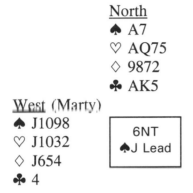

North
♠ A7
♡ AQ75
♢ 9872
♣ AK5

West (Marty)
♠ J1098
♡ J1032
♢ J654
♣ 4

6NT
♠J Lead

With my lovely spade sequence, the opening lead is no problem — I choose the ♠J. Declarer wins with dummy's ace, partner contributing the two. South now continues with the ♣AK as partner follows with the two and six. The time has come for my first, but not last, discard.

I do not want to discard a spade; that could set up declarer's fourth card if he began with KQxx. I don't want to discard a red card, either; I would like to retain my length in each of dummy's four-card suits. Not only am I stuck for a discard here, but I'm afraid more clubs are on their way. "Wow, what a nightmare."

Fortunately, I wake up. Thank goodness, it really was a nightmare. I don't have to make any discards. (Some would refer to this as an imaginative avoidance play on my part.)

What is the answer? Although not all bridge problems are solvable, this one is. (If you cannot wait, the answer is on page 172.)

One element of knowing what to discard is understanding *parity*: A defender must preserve the same number of cards that declarer or dummy holds to prevent declarer from winning a trick based on length. Invariably, the key number of cards is four. Defenders must avoid discarding from potentially useful four-card suits.

Consider the following deal, adapted from George Rosenkranz's article in the September 1990 issue of *The Bulletin*:

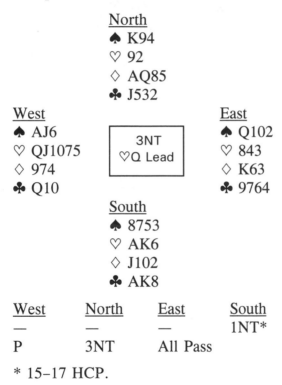

North
♠ K94
♡ 92
♢ AQ85
♣ J532

West
♠ AJ6
♡ QJ1075
♢ 974
♣ Q10

3NT
♡Q Lead

East
♠ Q102
♡ 843
♢ K63
♣ 9764

South
♠ 8753
♡ AK6
♢ J102
♣ AK8

West	North	East	South
—	—	—	1NT*
P	3NT	All Pass	

* 15–17 HCP.

Declarer won the ♡Q lead with his king, although he could have held up. He then led the ◇J for the losing finesse. East won his king and fired back the ♡8, which declarer ducked. West won with the ten and returned the jack to the ace, as declarer discarded a spade from dummy.

Declarer cashed three more rounds of diamonds. The spotlight turned to East as he considered his discard on the last diamond. Having not read this article (his real sin), East was not well versed on the subject of parity. Reluctant to release a spade, he discarded what he regarded as a useless club. Declarer and West each threw spades. When the diamond finesse lost, Declarer seemed destined for defeat. He shrugged and cashed his top clubs, with very gratifying results.

When the ♣Q fell, both clubs in dummy became winners. With East holding only the singleton nine, dummy's J5 were good for two tricks. Making 3NT made South's day, thanks to East's not keeping parity.

Answer to Nightmare

I do not like our chances of defeating 6NT if declarer has the ♡K. The only real hope is that the cards are distributed as follows:

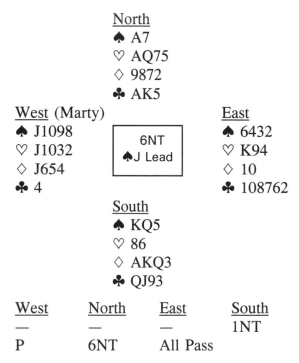

North
- ♠ A7
- ♡ AQ75
- ◇ 9872
- ♣ AK5

West (Marty)
- ♠ J1098
- ♡ J1032
- ◇ J654
- ♣ 4

6NT
♠J Lead

East
- ♠ 6432
- ♡ K94
- ◇ 10
- ♣ 108762

South
- ♠ KQ5
- ♡ 86
- ◇ AKQ3
- ♣ QJ93

West	North	East	South
—	—	—	1NT
P	6NT	All Pass	

I led the ♠J, which declarer won in dummy with the ace. He cashed the ♣A and ♣K, partner following up the line. Time to find a discard.

My best chance is to keep all of my diamonds, discarding hearts, then spades. Now, declarer is unable to take more than his 11 top tricks.

Accentuate the Negative

"Should I discard a high card in the suit that I want led, or a low one in the suit I don't?"

Although many players prefer to encourage in their strong suit, a better method is available, especially against notrump contracts. Preserve length in your good suit, hoping to win as many tricks as possible. You can easily afford to discard in your weak suit. After all, why keep garbage? At the risk of misquoting a leading psychiatrist, my advice is: **"Instead of accentuating the positive, discard the negative(s)."**

It is crucial for West to appreciate this concept on the following hand. You lead the ♠Q against 3NT.

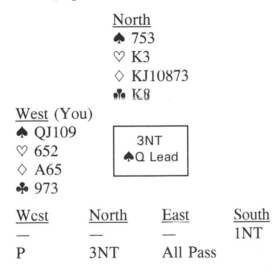

North
♠ 753
♡ K3
◇ KJ10873
♣ K8

West (You)
♠ QJ109
♡ 652
◇ A65
♣ 973

3NT
♠Q Lead

West	North	East	South
—	—	—	1NT
P	3NT	All Pass	

With the appearance of dummy's diamonds, prospects appear bleak for the defense. Partner's first card is the ♠2 as declarer wins the king. Before play continues, it is time for the *mandatory* trick-one counting of points. You have seven and dummy has 10, a total of 17. The opponents are playing 16–18 point notrumps, so declarer has at least 16. Therefore, partner has at most seven (40−33 = 7).

At trick two, declarer continues with the ◇Q; too bad, you were hoping partner had that card. You hold up as East plays the ◇4.

Declarer continues with the ♢9 at trick three, and again you play low. Unfortunately, there is no hope of isolating dummy's diamonds; one of those kings must be an entry (partner cannot have both missing aces with his maximum of seven points). However, you desperately want to see a discard or two from partner. He follows suit as declarer wins in dummy.

At trick four, declarer leads a third diamond from dummy and partner discards the ♡7. Declarer throws the ♠6 and you win the ♢A. The ♡7 appears to be low; the 2, 3, 5 and 6 are all in view. Now the spotlight shines brightly on you. What do you lead at trick five?

After partner's negative signal of the deuce at trick one, declarer must have the ♠A. Declarer has nine winners: five diamond tricks, two spades, and two more in the suit in which his ace sits opposite dummy's king. Therefore, the spade suit is not the answer; you must find and run partner's strong suit.

It is possible that partner began with ♡AQJ74 and has tried to encourage in that suit. However, knowing that discards should be treated negatively, you shift to a club. How does this work out?

Here is the entire hand:

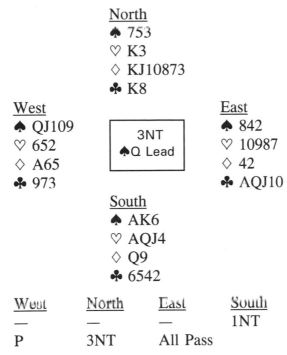

North
♠ 753
♡ K3
♢ KJ10873
♣ K8

West
♠ QJ109
♡ 652
♢ A65
♣ 973

3NT
♠Q Lead

East
♠ 842
♡ 10987
♢ 42
♣ AQJ10

South
♠ AK6
♡ AQJ4
♢ Q9
♣ 6542

West	North	East	South
—	—	—	1NT
P	3NT	All Pass	

You should appreciate that discouraging in hearts was partner's only hope of defeating the contract. Discarding a high club would have made it obvious for you to lead clubs. However, throwing away a winning card would also end any chance of taking four club tricks — a classic case of *winning the battle, but losing the war*. If you would like an easier way to win the war, please read on.

Improve Your Discards — Even the Odds

Standard discards serve as attitude signals — high cards encourage, low cards discourage. Unfortunately, these methods are often inadequate. Consider the following situations:

1. How do you show interest with AQ32?

2. How do you deny interest with 1098?

3. What do you do when you cannot afford to discard in the suit you want led (e.g., you hold AQJ, KQ10)?

Problems, problems! There is a better way. On your first discard, play an odd card to encourage. An even card would discourage and imply suit preference. This proven discarding technique is known as *odd-even discards* (*Roman discards*). Odd-even discards allow great flexibility. Most players take to them as easily as ducks do to water!

Odd-even discarding is an example of a convention involving signals. Yes, there are conventions for defense just as there are for bidding. Defensive carding agreements must be announced (and explained, if requested) before play begins.

Try the following hand. You are East and the opponents bid briskly to 4♠. You try to *will* partner to lead a diamond, but he leads the ♠A.

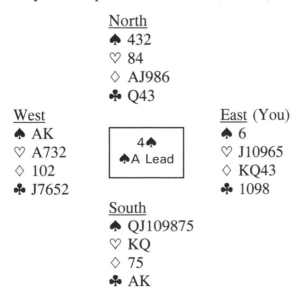

```
                    North
                    ♠ 432
                    ♡ 84
                    ◇ AJ986
                    ♣ Q43
     West                          East (You)
     ♠ AK        ┌──────────┐      ♠ 6
     ♡ A732      │   4♠     │      ♡ J10965
     ◇ 102       │ ♠A Lead  │      ◇ KQ43
     ♣ J7652     └──────────┘      ♣ 1098
                    South
                    ♠ QJ109875
                    ♡ KQ
                    ◇ 75
                    ♣ AK
```

West	North	East	South
—	—	—	1♠
P	2♠	P	4♠
All Pass			

After winning the first trick, partner continues with the trump king. Using standard signals, your most helpful discard would be the ♡5, discouraging hearts. You would prefer to signal with a high diamond, but you don't have one. A club discard is out of the question; you certainly don't want to encourage that suit.

Thanks to odd-even discards, you can easily encourage diamonds by discarding the ◊3, an odd-numbered card. However, consider the ♡10. As an even card, it discourages hearts. In addition, its status as a high spot card allows you to express your preference for diamonds, the higher-ranking of the other two suits. How convenient to have this option. The ♡10 discard would be crucial if your ◊3 was an even-numbered diamond spot; then it would be the only way to ask for a diamond switch.

You select the ♡10; preferring to tell partner about your holding in two suits at once. Partner looks that over, and loyally shifts to the ◊10. Since the clubs are blocked, declarer is helpless. He cannot use dummy's ♣Q to discard his diamond loser. When he plays dummy's ◊J, you win your queen and return a heart for the setting trick.

"Thanks for your signal, partner," says West. "Without that discard, diamonds is the last suit I would have attacked."

When armed with odd-even discards, you can triumph in many difficult defensive situations:

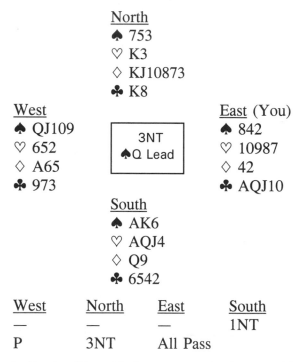

North
♠ 753
♡ K3
◇ KJ10873
♣ K8

West
♠ QJ109
♡ 652
◇ A65
♣ 973

3NT
♠Q Lead

East (You)
♠ 842
♡ 10987
◇ 42
♣ AQJ10

South
♠ AK6
♡ AQJ4
◇ Q9
♣ 6542

West	North	East	South
—	—	—	1NT
P	3NT	All Pass	

If this looks familiar, it's because we looked at this deal earlier in the chapter. Now you hold the East cards. Declarer wins the ♠Q lead with the king, as you play the deuce. He plays three rounds of diamonds until West wins his ace. On the third diamond, you need to find a discard that will tell partner what to do.

Now that you are familiar with odd-even discards, look how easy it becomes for you to announce your magnificent clubs. Your first discard will be the ♠4, clearly a low card since you played the two at trick one. You are discouraging spades while showing strength in clubs, the lower of the two remaining suits. No muss, no fuss — and so much easier than worrying about how partner will interpret the ♡7.

Odd-even discards are far superior to standard discards, and with a little practice they will be easy to use. They are also a great deal of fun. Try them; only declarer will be sorry!

CHAPTER 19
Opening Leads: Stop, Look, and Listen

Lead Trumps When You Are *Not* in Doubt

Everyone has heard the defensive maxim, "When in doubt, lead trumps." This is about as valuable as most other generalizations.

It's true you should sometimes lead trumps with unattractive holdings in the side suits. For example, with this hand and auction:

	LHO	Partner	RHO	You
♠ 64	—	—	1♠	Dbl
♡ AJ93	2♠	P	4♠	All Pass
◇ AQ105				
♣ KJ6	You would lead a trump.			

After the opening lead, the defenders will usually be eager to lead trumps when dummy has a short side suit. Frequently, however, it will be too late. It would be nice if you could have seen dummy before leading. Although this is not part of the rules, on some hands the bidding does enable the defense to make an *in-sight-ful* opening lead.

A great time to lead trumps is when dummy denies support for a major-suit opening bid. One example would be:

LHO	Partner	RHO	You
—	—	1♡/1♠	P
1NT	P	2◇	All pass

Responder obviously has fewer than three cards (0, 1 or 2) in opener's major. Can't you *see* that short suit?

The following auction screams for a trump lead. Unfortunately, West did not hear it. Do you?

North
♠ 6
♡ AJ109
◇ Q654
♣ Q864

West
♠ KJ93
♡ 75
◇ K87
♣ J1092

```
┌─────────┐
│   4♡    │
│ ??? Lead│
└─────────┘
```

East
♠ 1054
♡ 642
◇ A109
♣ K753

South
♠ AQ872
♡ KQ83
◇ J32
♣ A

West	North	East	South
—	P	P	1♠
P	1NT	P	2♡
P	3♡	P	4♡
All Pass			

Most players would lead the ♣J without thinking twice — what could be better than leading top of a sequence in an unbid suit? After this lead, it is easy for declarer to crossruff as follows: Win the ♣A and cash the ♠A. Ruff a spade, ruff a club, etc. Declarer ends up taking two aces and all eight trumps separately for ten tricks.

The defenders were poised to lead trumps after viewing dummy, but they had squandered their opportunity. Dummy's singleton spade should have come as no surprise. It was clear from the auction that declarer would need to ruff spade losers in dummy. West should have ignored his attractive club sequence and started by shortening North's trumps.

What happens after an opening trump lead? There is no longer any way for declarer to make the hand. A crossruff will now yield only nine tricks because the opening lead exhausted a trump from each hand. Two aces plus seven trump winners leaves declarer one trick short.

If your opening leads are based solely on your own hand, you are missing the boat. Your eyes may provide a vital sense, but for a bridge player, a well-tuned ear is essential.

Suitable and Stylish, Too

When it is not right to lead a trump, you will have three suits from which to choose. Two areas of confusion are leads in suits which include the ace and short-suit leads.

1. Leads in suits which include the ace:

    a) Never underlead an ace against a suit contract at trick one.
    b) If you do not have the king, lead an ace only when:
       - You are defending against a slam (except 6NT).
       - Declarer preempted.
       - Your ace is singleton.
       - Your ace is in the only unbid suit against 5♣ or 5◊.
       - Your side promised length and strength in the suit.
       - You have a seven or eight-card suit. (By the way, why aren't *you* declarer?).
    c) After trick one, lead the *king* from AK.

2. Short-suit leads:

    a) Singletons are invariably good choices.
    b) Doubletons are overrated, especially with one honor.
    c) The best time to lead a short suit is with trump control, e.g., A63.
    d) Avoid a short-suit lead:
       - When you do not need a ruff; e.g., with trump holdings such as QJ9 and KQ10.
       - When you have trump length. With four trumps it is usually correct to lead a long suit to make declarer ruff. This is an example of *the forcing game*.

A Good Lead is All You Need

On every bridge deal, the play begins with the opening lead. The fate of most contracts is at stake. In selecting your lead, you must consider your hand as well as inferences from the bidding.

The advantage of the opening lead was designated to the defense to allow them to select the first suit played. These questions and answers are intended to help you make the most of that advantage.

1. *What are the most desirable leads?*

   a) Partner's suit, especially if he promised five or six cards. The proper card to lead is the same one you would have led in any other suit. Therefore, lead low from Q63 or K852.
   b) Top of a three-card (or longer) sequence.

2. *Can you tell me more about sequences?*

   a) **It is better to lead top of a sequence than fourth-best.**
   b) A sequence must contain an honor (remember, the 10 is an honor). A holding of 7654 is not a sequence, it is consecutive garbage.
   c) Against a suit contract, a sequence can be as short as two cards. Lead the king from KQ53, and the queen from QJ64. However, against a notrump contract, lead low from both those holdings.

3. *Partner has not bid and I do not have a sequence. What now?*

   Prefer to lead a suit the opponents have not shown. In general, try to lead from length against any contract. A lead from Q1074 is more attractive than one from Q107. By the way, **it is acceptable to lead away from a king against a suit contract**.

4. *What about leading dummy's suit?*

   Leading through strength is overrated. Lead dummy's suit only when partner is likely to have length and strength behind him.

   Last, but definitely not least, no matter how badly partner's lead has worked out, do not sigh or make a face.

Watson, I Just Got a Lead

"Bridge is more than just a card game. It is a cerebral sport. Bridge teaches you logic, reasoning, quick thinking, patience, concentration and partnership skills."

Martina Navratilova (tennis is not her only racket)

Like a detective, a bridge player must uncover all the evidence needed to solve a problem. Paying attention to everything that happens during the bidding and play of a bridge hand is the trademark of a good sleuth.

An experienced player continuously collects clues. Because both sides are communicating through their bidding and play, information is always available. Unfortunately, most players fail to notice all the clues. Even fewer can apply what they have seen and heard.

Good bridge players also observe what did *not* happen at the table. For example, if you open the bidding after three passes and eventually become declarer, what do you know? Neither opponent has 13 points, nor is it likely that your RHO has 11 or 12; he would have opened light in third seat. If you need to locate an honor during the play, this information may be crucial.

Here is another illustration of deductive reasoning at the table:

North
♠ J2
♡ Q10
◇ AJ753
♣ QJ84

West (You)
♠ Q107
♡ 862
◇ 98
♣ AK765

5◇
♣A Lead

West	North	East	South
—	—	—	1◇
P	3◇*	P	5◇
All Pass			

* Limit raise.

You lead the ♣A, which declarer ruffs. He then draws two rounds of trumps. You began with two, dummy tabled five, and partner discarded on the second round, which accounts for eight trumps. Therefore, declarer began with five diamonds. Before going any further, try to figure out declarer's distribution in the major suits.

Declarer began with five diamonds and no clubs, so he must have eight major-suit cards. If they were divided 5–3 or 6–2, South would have opened with a 1♡ or 1♠. His major-suit distribution must be 4–4.

Of course, once you know the shape of declarer's hand, the only skill required to know partner's distribution is basic arithmetic. You have three spades and dummy has tabled two. When you add those five to declarer's four, you *know* that partner has four spades. Now you can do the same for hearts. Here is the entire hand:

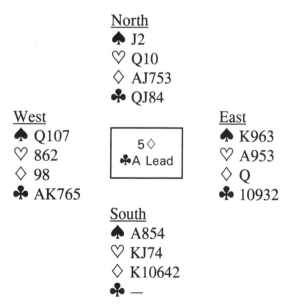

North
♠ J2
♡ Q10
♢ AJ753
♣ QJ84

West
♠ Q107
♡ 862
♢ 98
♣ AK765

5♢
♣A Lead

East
♠ K963
♡ A953
♢ Q
♣ 10932

South
♠ A854
♡ KJ74
♢ K10642
♣ —

Try another example to see if you possess some of Sherlock Holmes's powers of deduction. Again, you are West. It will not be difficult for you to go quietly, as you are gazing at:

	You	North	East	South
♠ 8632	—	—	—	1NT
♡ 874	P	2♣	P	2♡
◊ 92	P	3NT	All Pass	
♣ 7653				

Sherlock and I believe that there is a stand-out lead. Are you with us?

Because you have no good suit, you are going to attempt to find partner's. What do you know? Declarer's 2♡ bid promised four hearts, so a heart lead is out. The only reason for responder to bid Stayman is to locate a 4–4 major-suit fit. Since he did not raise opener's heart bid, he must have four spades. So much for the unbid major.

Many players progress this far and lead a club, the longer suit that neither opponent has shown. However, I believe those players are missing the boat. Sometimes your ears are more helpful than your eyes. In the famous Sherlock Holmes case, *Silver Blaze*, the key clue in unraveling the mystery was that the dog did *not* bark in the night. Who is that helpful canine in our scenario? It is your partner, of course.

With a very good club holding such as KQJ42, AK982, or even QJ1094, partner should have doubled the Stayman bid for a club lead. Since partner did *not* double 2♣, your best chance to get lucky is in diamonds. Lead your ◊9 and hope that destiny smiles upon you.

Nervous But Game
By Shelley Fehrenbach

I remember quite clearly the very first time,
    I played in a duplicate game.
My nerves were shattered, I began to shake,
    would I ever be the same?
My partner and I had prepared and rehearsed,
    we practiced each night on the phone.
We both knew the names Stayman and Michaels,
    as well as we knew our own.
I peered at my hand and was pleased to see,
    good shape and a long spade suit.
But as I made my 2♠ bid I gulped,
    no honors — only four points to boot.
My partner raised my bid to four,
    our defeat was painfully clear.
I tried to smile and look in control,
    though I prayed I would soon disappear.
I remembered what our teacher had said,
    the very day before.
"If you really mess up," he gently proclaimed,
    "don't throw your cards on the floor...
Don't make excuses and try to explain,
    or expect everyone to agree.
Just finish the hand, count up your tricks,
    and blame the auction on me."
As it turned out, we made our 4♠,
    the only East-West to go plus.
"The contract belonged to North-South in 4♡,"
    our opponents shouted at us.
"Since when do you open a spade suit like yours,"
    North screamed, "Don't you know how to play?"
"Well Marty Bergen taught us 'Points, schmoints,'
    so non-vul my suit seemed okay."
I thought South would snicker or do something worse,
    after all, I was a bit light..
But she said in a newly respectful tone,
    "If Marty said it — it must be right."

GLOSSARY

Ace from Ace-King Lead — The traditional lead of the king from AKx has been abandoned by many players in favor of the ace. This resolves the ambiguity for third hand as to whether opener is leading from the ace-king or king-queen. (Lead the king from AKx *after* trick one.)

Advance Sacrifice — A bid made before the opponents reach their optimum contract. The sacrifice is above the opponents' projected bid.

Alert — Attention drawn to an artificial bid or call.

American Contract Bridge League (ACBL) — The governing body for organized bridge activities and promotion in North America.

Artificial (Conventional) Bid — See Convention.

Attitude Signals — Carding used by a defender to encourage the suit led or to suggest a switch. Traditionally, this is achieved by playing a high card to encourage and low to discourage.

Auction — The bidding by the four players for the contract. The auction ends after three consecutive passes.

Avoidance Play — Declarer's plan of play designed to prevent a particular defender from gaining the lead.

Balanced Distribution — A hand with no singleton or void, and at most one doubleton. Balanced patterns are 4-4-3-2, 4-3-3-3, and 5-3-3-2.

Balancing Seat — A player is said to be in the balancing seat when his pass would end the auction. One should try to reopen with a bid or double rather than allow the opponents to play in a low-level contract.

Bennett Murder — Infamous incident in 1929 when a woman shot and killed her husband after he failed to make a 4♠ contract. (See page 35.)

Bergen Raises — Convention that allows responder to define his strength and precise number of trumps in support of partner's 1♡ or 1♠ opening.

Blackwood — Very popular convention in which a 4NT bid is used to discover the number of aces partner holds.

Blocked Suit — A suit in which entry problems make it difficult or impossible to cash winners. For example, AQ opposite Kxx.

Board — Dummy's hand. *On the board* means in dummy's hand. This also refers to the physical board in which the cards are placed.

Call — The correct term for all possible actions taken during the bidding. Pass, double, redouble, 1♠ (etc.) are all *call*s.

Card Sense — A special aptitude for playing card games, specifically (in this context) bridge.

Cash — To lead a winning card and take the trick.

Cheapest Bid — The most economical bid available at any particular point in the auction, such as 1♢ over 1♣.

Cheapest of Equals — Third hand's play of the lowest card that will prevent declarer from winning a cheap undeserved trick. An example would be playing the J from QJx.

Checkback Stayman — Similar to *new minor forcing*. After opener rebids 1NT, a bid of 2♣ by responder asks about opener's major suits.

Clear a Suit — At notrump, forcing out the opponents' high cards so that the remaining cards in the suit are winners. At suit play, the elimination of all cards in a suit from both the declarer's and dummy's hand.

Cold — Slang term describing an easily makeable contract. *Frigid* and *laydown* are equivalent terms. In postmortem discussions, players tend to exaggerate the degree of coldness in contracts played by others.

Competitive Auction — An auction where both sides are bidding.

Concede — During the play of a hand, to yield one or more of the remaining tricks to the defenders.

Constructive Auction — An auction where only one side is bidding; i.e., a noncompetitive auction.

Contract — (n) The final bid of the auction. (v) The process of winning the bid to become the declaring side.

Control — A holding (ace, king, singleton or void) that prevents the opponents from winning the first two tricks in a suit.

Convention — A call or play with a defined meaning understood by the partnership. It may bear little resemblance to the natural meaning of the bid. The most popular conventions are *Stayman* and *Blackwood*.

Convention Card — In duplicate bridge, the card listing the system and conventions used by the partnership.

Counting — Separates the bridge players from the BRIDGE PLAYERS. Good players count: trump, distribution, high cards, tricks, etc.

Count Signal — Carding used by the defenders to communicate their length when declarer leads a suit. This assumes that the defender is not involved in competing for the trick. Signal with the highest card you can afford from an even number of cards. Play low with an odd number.

Covering Honors — When an honor is led and the opponent follows with a higher honor, he is said to have covered an honor with an honor. Average players tend to do so too often.

Crossruff — A method of play where both partners ruff. The best defense against a crossruff is leading trumps. Declarer should cash his side-suit winners ASAP.

Cuebid — An artificial, forcing bid in the opponent's suit. Also a bid of a new suit — after the trump suit has been established — as a slam try.

Deal — (n) All four hands, i.e., all 52 cards. (v) To distribute the cards to the four players.

Defensive Bidding — Bidding by the side that did not open.

Denomination — The correct technical term for notrump and suits.

Develop — To make a suit or an individual card good by forcing out an opponent's higher card(s). Good players develop, average players grab. A bridge synonym for develop is *establish*.

Direct Seat — Position in which a player's RHO has just made a bid.

Discard — (n) A card played when void in the suit led. (v) To play a non-trump card when void in the suit led. (Otherwise it's a *revoke*.) Colloquialisms for discard are *pitch, ditch, sluff* and *shake*.

Discovery Play — A play made to learn more about the concealed hands.

Distribution — The number of cards held in each suit.

Distribution Points — The total of HCP plus short-suit points.

DONT — Disturb Opponent's Notrump, a.k.a Bergen Over Notrump. Emphasizes distribution, not points. With a two-suited hand, overcall in your lower-ranking suit. Double with a one-suited hand.

Double — The most important call in bridge. The two main categories are penalty and takeout. Players must be able to distinguish between the two.

Down — Defeated; said of a contract that fails.

Drawing Trump — Playing trumps until the opponents run out.

Drury — Convention in which a 2♣ response to a third or fourth-seat opening of 1♡ or 1♠ promises support for the major and a maximum passed hand.

Duck — To play a small card, surrendering a trick you might have won. Most players do not duck often enough.

Duke of Cumberland Hand — A sensational historic hand where one side made a grand slam although an opponent held 31 HCP and KJ9 of trumps! Immortalized by Ian Fleming in *Moonraker*. (See page 6.)

Duplicate Bridge — A form of bridge in which the same deal is played by many different pairs. Poor-card holders are not punished.

Echo — The play of a high card, then a low card in a suit.

Endplay (Throw-in Play) — Declarer deliberately puts a defender on lead at a key moment and applies *Last is Best*.

Entry — A holding that provides access to a hand. Efficient use of entries is crucial for both sides.

Equal Vulnerability — Situation in which both sides are vulnerable or both nonvulnerable.

Establish — See **Develop**.

Expert — A player of proven ability. The caliber of the player accorded this title will vary with the circles in which he plays.

Favorable Vulnerability — Not vulnerable versus vulnerable opponents, also called *white against red*. The favorite vulnerability of all duplicate players. The best time for very aggressive competitive bidding.

Feature — Ace or king of a side (not trump) suit. Commonly shown by opener after a 2NT response to his opening weak two-bid.

Finesse — A technique used in an attempt to win a trick with a card that is not presently a winner. A successful finesse takes advantage of the favorable location of the opponent's card(s).

Fit — A term referring to the partnership's combined assets, often with respect to a suit, usually trump.

Five-Bagger — A five-card suit. Similarly, a six-bagger is acceptable slang for a six-card suit, etc.

Five-Card Majors — A bidding style in which 1♡ or 1♠ is opened with at least five cards in the suit. Especially popular in the United States.

Forcing Bid — A bid that partner must not pass. Some forcing bids do not promise strength. For example, after 1♣ – P – 1♡ – P, opener must bid again even though responder *might* have only six points.

Forcing Game — Defensive strategy of leading a suit to force declarer to ruff (or lose the trick). Aimed at shortening declarer's trumps in the hope that one defender will gain control with a master trump. A very effective technique. See **Trump Promotion**.

Forcing Raise — After a 1♡ or 1♠ opening, an artificial response of 3NT. This shows a strong raise with 13–16 distributional points. Many duplicate players use Jacoby 2NT as their *forcing raise*, which keeps the bidding at a lower level. Opener must not pass. A limit jump raise (i.e., 1♠-P-3♠) would not be forcing.

Fourth-Best Lead — Traditionally, when lacking a sequence, the fourth-highest card is led. This allows partner (and declarer) to apply The Rule of 11. For example, with K9842, lead the four.

Fourth-Suit Game Forcing — Artificial bid of the fourth (unbid) suit that commits the partnership to at least a game contract.

Free Bid — A bid made when partner and RHO have taken action. In modern bidding, it does not guarantee additional strength.

Free Finesse — A defensive lead that eliminates a possible loser for declarer. Often a result of an endplay. Obviously, everyone's favorite type of finesse. For example, LHO leads into declarer's AQ suit.

Game Forcing — A bid made by either member of the partnership that commits them to bid game, with slam a possibility.

Garbage Stayman (Weak Stayman) — Stayman bid with a weak hand short in clubs. Responder usually intends to pass opener's rebid.

Gerber — Convention that asks for aces after partner's notrump bid. When 4NT would be quantitative (not Blackwood), 4♣ inquires about partner's aces. Partner answers 4♢ to show zero or four aces, 4♡ shows one; 4♠ shows two; 4NT shows three.

Good Shape — A hand is said to have good shape when it has long and short suits. Hands which lack good shape are *balanced*.

HCP — High card points. In determining the high-card value of a hand, an ace is worth four points, a king three, a queen two and a jack one.

Hit — Slang used as two distinct verbs: 1) To double; 2) To ruff.

Hold-Up Play — Refusing to win a winnable trick, hoping to cut the opponents' communication.

Interior Sequence — Consecutive cards within a suit where the top card is not part of the sequence; for example, KJ109. The J109 is the interior sequence. The proper card to lead is the jack, not the nine.

Invitational Bid — A bid that encourages, but does not force, partner to go to game or slam.

Jacoby Transfer — Used in response to notrump opening bids, or a natural notrump overcall. A diamond bid promises heart length, while a heart response shows at least five spades. Opener must bid the suit responder has "shown." One of the most important modern conventions.

Jordan 2NT — After a double of partner's opening bid, a jump to 2NT promises 10 or more points with four trumps. Opener is now well placed to bid game or sign off in the agreed trump suit. Applies to opening bids in both majors and minors.

Jump Shift — A new-suit response one level higher than necessary. A jump shift by responder promises at least 17 points; by opener it indicates at least 19 points. Of course, both are forcing to game. Some duplicate players treat responder's jump shift as weak.

Kibitz — The act of watching a game. Kibitzers are expected to ask permission to observe, to watch only one hand at a time, and to remain silent, before, during and after a hand has been played. Yeah, right!

"Last is Best" — A crucial Bergenism that emphasizes the advantage enjoyed by the person playing last to a trick.

Law of Total Tricks ("The Law") — Helpful to players at all levels when judging whether to bid on in competitive auctions. Based on the concept that "Trump Length is Everything." Discovered by Jean-René Vernes, expanded by Marty Bergen, and popularized in Larry Cohen's classic book, *To Bid or Not to Bid*.

Lead-Directing Doubles — Doubles of artificial bids, promising length and strength in the suit named. Some examples are doubles of *Stayman*, *Jacoby transfers*, and responses to *Blackwood*.

LHO — Left-hand opponent; the player on your left.

Life Master — Status attained by duplicate players who have accumulated 300 masterpoints, some in regional or national tournaments.

Limit Raise — Responder's invitational raise from one to three of a suit, promising 11-12 distribution points and trump support.

Lose Control — When declarer can no longer make his contract because his opponents are able to win tricks in their long suit. In suit contracts, often the result of declarer running out of trumps.

Loser-on-Loser Play — Declarer's choice not to trump, preferring, instead, to discard an inevitable side-suit loser.

Masterpoint — A measure of achievement in duplicate play. Winning many masterpoints does not equate to bridge expertise.

Menace — see **Threat Card**.

Michaels Cuebid — An overcall in the opponent's suit that shows at least five cards in two other suits. The emphasis is on the unbid major(s).

Mirror Distribution — Said of a deal where partners have the same distribution in each of the four suits.

Misfit — Description of a situation where the partnership is unable to agree on a trump suit. You should stop bidding ASAP.

Mississippi Heart Hand — An infamous trick deal dating from the days of whist. Despite holding ♠ AKQ ♡ AKQJ109 ◇ — ♣ AKQJ, declarer can take only six tricks with hearts as trump! (See page 148.)

Negative Double — Responder's double after partner opens the bidding and RHO overcalls. It promises some values as well as length (four or more cards) in an unbid major. Absolutely essential for winning bridge.

New Minor Forcing — After opener's rebid of 1NT or 2NT, responder's bid in an unbid minor asks opener about his major-suit length. Responder usually has a five-card major with game-invitational values.

Odd-Even Discards — Discarding method where an odd-numbered card encourages, while an even-numbered card discourages and suggests suit preference. Also referred to as **Roman Discards**.

Off-Shape — Distribution partner will not expect.

1NT Forcing — Convention in which a 1NT response to partner's major-suit opening cannot be passed. This is often used in conjunction with *two-over-one game forcing*. Very popular among duplicate players, but not necessary for good bidding.

1NT Overcall — A bid of 1NT after RHO has opened. Shows a hand that would have opened 1NT, including a stopper in opener's suit.

Overcall — A bid made after an opponent has opened. Suit length and strength, level and vulnerability are crucial; your distribution and holding in the opponent's suit are also factors. *Points, schmoints!*

Overruff — Overtrumping your RHO.

Overtake — Play of a higher card than partner. You are either unblocking or intending to make a constructive lead.

Parity — A defender must preserve the same length that declarer or dummy holds in a suit.

Partscore — A contract less than game.

Penalty Double (Business Double) — A double of an opponent's bid that says, "I don't think you can make that contract." If the contract fails, the penalty will increase.

Pointed Suits — Spades and diamonds, so named because of their shape.

"Points, Schmoints" — A Bergenism that emphasizes trumps and shape, while de-emphasizing HCP.

Postmortem — A term applied to the discussion of bridge hands after the conclusion of play. The best part of some players' game.

Preemptive Bid — A jump bid made with a long suit and a weak hand. The intention is to usurp the opponents' bidding space, making it harder for them to reach their optimum contract.

Preference — When a player bids two suits, and his partner returns to the original suit at the lowest possible level. This promises no additional strength; in fact, a preference is no stronger than a pass.

Present Count (Remaining Count) — A defensive signal in which a player communicates the number of cards in a suit. See **Count Signal**.

Probability — A mathematical principle with many bridge applications. Players must be aware of the likely division of the opponents' cards.

Professional Player — Expert hired to play on teams, or in partnership with less experienced players who hope to learn and win.

Puppet Stayman — After a notrump opening, a response in clubs can be used to ask opener if he holds a four-card or five-card major.

Quantitative 4NT — A raise of partner's notrump bid to four *invites* a notrump slam. It does *not* ask partner how many aces he holds.

Quick Trick — A high-card holding that will usually result in a fast trick on defense. AK = 2 quick tricks; AQ = 1½, A or KQ = 1, Kx = ½.

Raise — Supporting partner's suit (or notrump).

Rebid — (n) A player's second bid of the auction. (v) To repeat a bid in the same suit, promising extra length.

Rebiddable suit — A suit of at least six cards. It is usually incorrect to rebid an unsupported five-card suit.

Redouble — A call allowed only after an opponent has doubled. The most common redouble occurs after partner's opening bid is doubled. Now, responder's redouble promises at least 10 points.

Remaining Count — See **Present Count**.

Responder — Partner of the opening bidder.

Responsive Double — A type of takeout double that occurs after the opponents have bid and raised and partner has taken action.

Resultor — A player (or kibitzer) whose analysis is based on having seen all four hands. Many players result better than they play. Only a mother would love a resultor.

Reverse — Opener's rebid at the two-level in a higher-ranking suit than his first bid shows at least 17 points and promises five or six cards in his first suit. This topic causes more anxiety than any other one.

Revoke — Failure of a player to follow suit when he is not void. A penalty is assessed against the offending side.

RHO — Right-hand opponent; the player to your right.

Rounded Suits — Hearts and clubs; based on their shape.

Ruff — To play a trump when you are void in a suit.

Ruff and Sluff — When a defender leads a suit in which both declarer and dummy are void, declarer can trump (ruff) in one hand and discard (sluff) a loser from the other. When declarer has trumps in each hand and a losing card, a ruff-sluff will prove beneficial. It is also possible for declarer to give the defenders a ruff-sluff.

Ruffing Finesse — A finesse in which one player is void. For example, with KQJ10 opposite a void, an honor would be led. If the opponent covers with the ace, declarer will ruff. If the opponent plays low, declarer can discard a loser. In either case, three tricks are established in the suit.

Ruffing Value — Dummy's short side suit. Declarer hopes to ruff his losers with dummy's trumps.

Rule of 11 — Applied to fourth-best leads. The numerical value of the card led is subtracted from 11; the difference represents the number of higher cards held by the other three players.

Rule of 15 — A formula used to determine if a player in fourth seat should open with a borderline hand. Spades are the key. If the sum of HCP plus number of spades totals 15 or more, open the bidding.

Rule of 20 — Used to evaluate whether to open borderline hands in first and second seat. Add the length of your two longest suits to your HCP. With 20 or more, open the bidding in a suit at the one-level.

Sacrifice — A bid made with no expectation of making the contract. The player hopes to lose fewer points than the opponents would have scored if allowed to play in their contract.

Sandwich Overcall — An overcall made after both opponents have bid.

Second Hand Low — The play of a small card when RHO leads, based on the fact that partner still has a turn.

Sequence — In notrump, three consecutive cards containing at least one honor. In suit contracts, two consecutive cards suffice. Prefer leading the top of the sequence to fourth-best. At notrump, it is also correct to lead the queen from QJ98 or king from KQ106, etc.

Short Club — Those players who require a four-card suit to open 1♢ are occasionally forced to open 1♣ with only two cards. This practice is far more popular with the masses than with their expert counterparts.

Short-Suit Points — Used in suit contracts to evaluate a hand: three points for a void; two for a singleton; and one for a doubleton. With four-card support, add an additional point for each singleton or void.

Side Suit — A suit of at least four cards, other than trumps.

Signal — Defensive play used to exchange information about the hand.

Sign-Off Bid — A bid intended to end the auction. Sometimes referred to as a *drop-dead bid*.

Sluff — See **Discard.**

Solid Suit — A suit where no losers are likely. AKQJ109 is 100% solid, while AKQJ32 is probably solid.

SOS Redouble — A redouble for rescue, asking partner to retreat to another suit. Handle with care — this only applies when there is no possibility that partner will interpret the redouble as strength-showing.

Splinter Raise — Conventional jump into a short suit (0 or 1 card), promising good support for partner and values for game or slam.

Split — The manner in which a suit divides.

Splitting Honors — Defender's play of an honor in second position from two or more sequential honor cards.

Spot Cards — Cards two through nine. Diagramed in bridge hands as *x*.

Squeeze — A series of plays that forces a defender to part with a winner. Declarer's best hope when he holds one seemingly inevitable loser.

Stayman — The response of 2♣ to 1NT, or 3♣ to 2NT, asking opener to bid a four-card major suit. Opener bids 2◊ to deny a major.

Stiff — Acceptable slang for a singleton.

Stopper — A card or combination of cards that prevents the opponents from running a suit in a notrump contract.

Suit-Preference Signal — A card played by a defender to direct his partner to lead a specific suit. Most often used when a player hopes to give his partner a ruff.

Support — Raising partner's suit with adequate trumps.

Support Double — Opener doubles RHO's overcall of partner's one-level response to show three-card trump support.

Support With Support — Bergenism designed to remind players to raise when holding trump support.

Takeout Double — A double which asks partner to bid his best suit that has not been named by the opponent(s). In general, a double is defined as takeout if it is made: 1) before partner has bid; 2) early in the auction.

Team Game — A form of competition where teams of four to six players compete against each other. One pair sits East-West while their teammates play the same deals as North-South at the other table. Various team events include Swiss Teams, Knock-Out Teams and Board-a-Match.

Tenace — A combination of honors where the outcome is in doubt. Some examples are AQ and KJ. When holding a tenace, playing *last is best*.

Third Hand High — Used when competing for the trick in a suit led by partner. Play of a high card to prevent the opponents from winning a cheap, undeserved trick.

Threat Card (Menace) — A card that may become a winner if the opponents can be forced to discard that suit. The term is used primarily in connection with squeezes.

Throw-in Play — See **Endplay**.

Timing — The order in which trumps are pulled, losers are trumped, and side suits are developed. Crucial for both declarer and defenders.

Touching Suits — Suits which are next to one another from a bidding perspective. Clubs and diamonds, diamonds and hearts, hearts and spades and spades and clubs are said to be touching suits.

Trap Pass — A pass with a promising hand hoping to collect a sizeable penalty by defeating the opponent's contract.

Trump — (n) The suit named in the contract. Trumps always beat non-trumps. (v) See **Ruff**.

Trump Promotion — An extra trump trick created by the defense, often based on an overruff.

2♣ Opening — A strong, artificial and forcing opening bid used with powerhouse hands when playing weak-two bids. Opener either has a long suit, or a balanced hand too strong to open 2NT.

Two-Over-One Game Forcing — A modern bidding approach with many adherents. As an unpassed hand, responder's bid in a new suit at the two level promises an opening bid and commits the partnership to game.

Two-Suited Hand — A hand containing at least five cards in the longest suit and four or more in the second-longest.

Unbalanced Hand — A hand with a singleton, void or two doubletons.

Unbid Suit — Any suit not bid during the auction.

Unblock — The play of a high card in order to preserve a small card.

Unfavorable Vulnerability — Vulnerable versus nonvulnerable opponents a.k.a., *red against white*. Use discretion when overcalling or preempting.

Unmakeable — A contract which cannot succeed unless the defense slips.

Unusual NT Overcall — A method of showing length in the two lower unbid suits after an opponent opens at the one level. If an opponent opens a major, 2NT promises at least five cards in each minor.

Up the Line — The practice of bidding the cheapest suit when responding with *four*-card suits. Also said of defensive carding.

Uppercut — On defense, creating a trump trick through an overruff.

Vulnerability — Determines the game/slam bonus, or the size of the penalty for not fulfilling a contract. Relevant in many bidding decisions.

Weak Jump Overcall (WJO) — After RHO opens, a jump shows a weak hand with a long (6 cards or more), strong suit. It is very similar to a weak two-bid.

Weak Jump Raises (WJR) — An effective tool for preemptively raising partner's bid in a competitive auction. Based on *The Law of Total Tricks*.

Weak Jump Shift in Competition — In competitive auctions, the use of a jump response in a new suit to show a preemptive hand.

Weak Two-Bid — An opening preempt in diamonds, hearts or spades. The bid traditionally promises 5-10 HCP and a six-card suit headed by three of the top five honors.

Whist — The forerunner of bridge, with no bidding and no dummy.

Yarborough — A hand with no card above a nine.

INDEX

HIGHLY RECOMMENDED

Read more about it...

If you enjoyed *POINTS SCHMOINTS!* you might want to consider ordering one or more of the following publications. (Ordering details can be found on page 210.) Bridge books make a thoughtful gift for your card-playing friends and family, too. Thank you, and happy reading!

Hardcover Books by Marty Bergen

MARTY SEZ	$17.95
MARTY SEZ – VOLUME II	$17.95
POINTS SCHMOINTS!	$19.95
More *POINTS SCHMOINTS*!	$19.95
Schlemiel...Schlimazel? Mensch	$14.95

UNPRECEDENTED OFFER

If your purchase of Marty's hardcover books exceeds $25, you will automatically receive a 50% discount.

Autographs upon request.

Softcover Books by Marty Bergen

1NT Forcing	$4.95
Evaluate Your Hand Like an Expert	$4.95
Introduction to Negative Doubles	$6.95
Negative Doubles	$9.95
Better Bidding With Bergen 1 — Uncontested Auctions	$11.95
Better Bidding With Bergen 2 — Competitive Bidding	$11.95

CDs By Larry Cohen

Play Bridge With Larry Cohen – 1999 Life Master Pairs
An exciting opportunity to play question-and-answer with a
17-time national champion.

Day 1	~~$29.95~~	$26.00
Day 2	~~$29.95~~	$26.00
Day 3	~~$29.95~~	$26.00

FREE SHIPPING ON ALL SOFTWARE

Books by Eddie Kantar

A Treasury of Bridge Bidding Tips	$11.95
Take Your Tricks (Declarer Play)	$12.95
Defensive Tips for Bad Card Holders	$12.95

Unique Gift Suggestion

365 Bridge Hands with Expert Analysis	~~$13.95~~	$5.00

Software by Mike Lawrence

Counting at Bridge   ~~$34.95~~ $30.00
   Shows you ways to gather information and how to use it.

Private Bridge Lessons, Volume One   ~~$34.95~~ $30.00
   Declarer techniques that everybody needs to know.

Private Bridge Lessons, Volume Two   ~~$34.95~~ $30.00
   All new material. Over 100 hands with interactive feedback.

Defense   ~~$34.95~~ $30.00
   How to avoid errors and take as many tricks as possible.

Two Over One   ~~$34.95~~ $30.00
   Hundreds of hands to maximize your game and slam bidding.

Conventions   ~~$60.00~~ $48.00
   A must for every partnership.

FREE SHIPPING ON ALL SOFTWARE

ONE-ON-ONE WITH MARTY

Improve your bridge with an experienced, knowledgeable teacher. Enjoy a private bridge lesson with Marty Bergen. You choose the format and topics covered – including Q&A, conventions, bidding and cardplay.

Marty is available for bridge lessons via phone and e-mail. Beginners, intermediates and advanced players will all benefit from his clear and helpful teaching style.

For further information, please call Marty at 800-386-7432, or e-mail him at mbergen@mindspring.com

ORDERING INFORMATION

To place your order, please send a check or money order to:

Marty Bergen
9 River Chase Terrace
Palm Beach Gardens, FL 33418-6817

Credit card orders are also welcome.
1-800-386-7432

Please include $3 postage and handling (U.S. dollars).
Postage is free **if your order includes** *any of Marty's hardcover books*.